Appel
5112 Beachwood r
Beachwood, OH .

D0930491

Listen
to the
Soul

Chaim Walder

FELDHEIM PUBLISHERS JERUSALEM / NEW YORK

Listen To The Soul!

Stories
that touch the heart
and nurture the spirit

Translated by Devora Friedman
Edited by Aviva Rappaport

First impression 1996

ISBN 0- 87306-780-0

Originally published in Hebrew as
שימו לב אל הנשמה

Book Design by Aviva Rappaport

FELDHEIM PUBLISHERS
POB 35002 / Jerusalem, Israel

200 Airport Executive Park
Nanuet, NY 10954

Printed in Israel

"שִׂימוּ לֵב אֶל הַנְּשָׁמָה,
לְשֵׁם שְׁבוּ וְאַחְלָמָה,
וְאוֹרָהּ כְּאוֹר הַחַמָּה,
שִׁבְעָתַיִם כְּאוֹר הַבֹּקֶר."
(מתוך זמירות שבת)

"...כִּי הָאָדָם יִרְאֶה לַעֵינַיִם
וַה' יִרְאֶה לַלֵּבָב."
(שמואל א טז, ז)

Contents

In lieu of an introduction

B'ezras Hashem Yisborach I have been privileged to write and publish this volume, the third book of mine published to date — yet, in a certain way, the first.

Although most of my writing deals with the world of adults, my first two books dealt with the world of children, for my heart is drawn to that world.

In the introduction to my first book I wrote: "I am sure that every writer dreams of writing about a world better and truer than the one we live in. I found this magical world — a world so wonderful and pure, so gentle and sensitive — in the world of children.

"Writing for and about children," I continued, "comes from the depths of the heart, and it is a writing of love. Touching. Never hurtful."

Not many understood the cry behind these words. One who did understand, a well-known educator in Bnei Brak, wrote me: "Every child eventually leaves that magical world for the world you cry out against. His soul does not change but only becomes covered with layers which hide the innocence within. Remove those layers!"

That's when I knew that I would begin to listen to the soul, to penetrate to the depths of the human heart and examine what motivates it.

This contemplation was accomplished through the stories I wrote — stories that do not describe the world as it is but rather portray it as I would wish it to be.

As raw material for these same stories, I deliberately used inscrutable characters, people like Agon, the haughty grocery store owner; Shaya'le, the sarcastic critic; Mishkin, the Communist; Shlomo, the son who rebelled against his father and abandoned religion; Josh, Chaya Ita, and all the others.

These are the people who, at first glance, make us think what we do about the world. But a peek into the depths reveals that each and every person has a good pure soul, which is only hidden behind the scars of difficult events and disappointments.

In the mouths of these characters I have placed the words that explain much of what one needs to know about the human soul. I purposely put the clearest, most direct message into the mouth of the biggest thief, Heikin, who decided to become a better person after meeting the pure-hearted, pitiful yet faithful servant with the sterling character:

"Imagine how the world would look if there were a few more pure-hearted people like Onchik," said Heikin. "Would there be room for theft and corruption in such a world? Would anyone dare commit the deeds I used to?"

That is why I wrote this book.

❑ ❑ ❑

This is the place to mention those pure souls in whose merit I am able to write stories like these and indeed to write at all: My wife Bracha תחי׳, and my children Meir Zvi נ״י, Moshe נ״י, and David נ״י, who are like a crystal-clear sea of absolute good in whose depths can be easily be seen the positive and the pure in every creature with a soul.

Chaim Walder

Yachsente

When Chaya Ita came of age, the local matchmakers lost no time in offering her prospective marriage partners of the highest caliber. Knowing full well that it was pointless to propose an ordinary boy from a plain home, they racked their brains, some of them even combing the study halls around the country, for the prized *bachur* who would be as brilliant as the Gaon of Vilna, of as noble lineage as Yitzchak *Avinu*, as handsome as Yosef *HaTzaddik*, and possessing the character traits of Choni *HaMe'agel*.

You must understand — Chaya Ita was a genuine *"yachsente,"* a girl of real aristocratic lineage. Her father was none other than Reb Shaul, the head of the community, a dignified man both wealthy and learned at the very same time.

Nine of Reb Shaul's children had already established their own homes. His sons had married the daughters of prominent Torah scholars, and his sons-in-law were eminent rabbis and community leaders. Chaya Ita was his youngest child and the apple of his eye.

It was rumored that Chaya Ita was also the most gifted of all his daughters. All raved about her intelligence, refined manners and erudition. She could play the piano as well as design dresses for herself and her sisters. She was a rare blend, they said, of beauty, brains and *balebatishkeit* — and, let us not forget, a *yachsente!*

Shadchanim came and went in Reb Shaul's large home. Most of the offers made were rejected straight-away by Reb Shaul. Of the small number considered, in only a select few was permission granted to proceed.

Here, though, a problem was encountered which neither the *shadchanim* nor Reb Shaul had anticipated. It seems that these same select few were rejected straight off the bat, by whom, if not Chaya Ita herself!

One she rejected because he was "of poor intelligence," another because his views were "unreasonable," a third because his aspirations were "undefined," and a fourth because he was "hesitant and lacking in self-confidence."

Strange as it may seem, the young men Chaya Ita eventually did meet rejected her too — but for totally different reasons.

One claimed that his conversation with her had taken the form of an interview, in which he had been asked dozens of questions on various and sundry topics. Another complained that Chaya Ita had definite opinions about everything, which would not be so terrible in and of itself but the problem was, according to that same *bachur*, that Chaya Ita insisted that her conversational partner hold exactly the same views, and that she had some uncomplimentary expressions and descriptions for anyone who didn't. That very same *bachur* also ventured to surmise that if Chaya Ita was a pain in the neck for whoever engaged in conversation with her, how much more so she would be for anyone who married her.

The third rejected her without offering a reason. The fourth praised Chaya Ita's personality but added, "I'm looking for a wife, not a personality."

At first, Reb Shaul reproved the *shadchanim* and told them that they weren't making enough of an effort to find his daughter a suitable match. However, after a number of years had passed, during which dozens of young men had been rejected by, or had themselves rejected, Chaya Ita, Reb Shaul realized that he had a problem on his hands.

❧ Chapter Two: Menash'ke

It was the brash *shadchan*, Menash'ke, who had the audacity to say, "Reb Shaul, I suspect your daughter is looking for a *sefer* Torah or a prayer stand. Otherwise, the way she treats regular mortals who seek to marry her makes no sense."

Menash'ke was about the only one in the world capable of saying such a thing to a man like Reb Shaul. He was an interesting creature, this Menash'ke. Tall as a shoelace and with a voice a bit shrill, his pants waged a perpetual battle with his shoes, something that was quite understandable in light of the condition of the latter. No one but Menash'ke could tell a father: "Your son is as clever as a broken laundry pail!" After all, wasn't he Menash'ke the *shadchan*? Such remarks, and quite a few others like them, spilled forth from his mouth at a rate that wouldn't embarrass even...the average washerwoman.

Actually, Menash'ke was taking a calculated risk with his descriptions. Half of his listeners would throw him down the stairs. That's why Menash'ke was not particularly fond of suggesting matches to people who lived in houses with a lot of stairs. Rolling down them was not one of his favorite pastimes — or anyone else's, when you come to think of it.

The other half, though, would not throw Menash'ke down the stairs but would instead nod their heads and say, "Menash'ke, perhaps you're right. Perhaps you are even an angel sent by Heaven to rescue me from my troubles. Go ahead, then, and find a decent match for my son. But make sure that she at least knows that one does not place two feet in one boot."

At that point, his task would become easier, and in a relatively short time, Menash'ke would generally manage to conclude matches that had at the outset seemed lost causes, and thus help establish more Jewish homes.

The other *shadchanim* in town were sharply critical of Menash'ke's tactics. Some even dared to venture that they were downright shameful. In their opinion, the excessive pressure Menash'ke placed on his clients caused them to make sweeping compromises. Those same *shadchanim* even claimed that Menash'ke often failed to fulfill the conditions asked of him and would come forth with a bride who really knew nothing at all about boots.

Menash'ke, for his part, did not deny their charges at all. He said he had to do it that way, and that his main business and livelihood was based on the "touch-ups" he made when he related information about a client's character.

Menash'ke even bolstered his claim by saying that the word "*shadchan*" (whose Hebrew letters are *shin, daled, chaf,* and *nun*) is an acronym for "*sheker dover, kesef notel* — he tells you no truths and takes your money."

"Here's proof for you of the true nature of my occupation," he used to say.

❧ Chapter Three: Reb Shaul

However, after speaking so brashly to Reb Shaul, Menash'ke was not thrown out of the house. In fact, Reb

Shaul didn't even argue with him. He simply nodded his head and said, "You're right. I never should have encouraged her to be so choosy. Don't think I'm pleased with her reasons for rejecting each and every prospect. To tell you the truth, every now and then, I also tell her that her demands are unrealistic.

"But with each passing day, I grow more desperate. *Shadchanim* have made hundreds of proposals, offering her the finest young men in the country but to no avail. She's rejected every single one of them.

"Hashem has blessed me with a clever daughter. But did she have to be *so* clever?"

Nu. Menash'ke had nothing to add. He was bewildered to the roots of his beard by Reb Shaul's rare display of candor. It took a while for him even to recall why he had come. "I have someone for her, a *shidduch* she'll pursue as far as China," he said at last, murmuring his standard preamble to every proposal he made, even though he hadn't the faintest idea where said China was. "Do you know the eminent *dayan* of . . . ?"

She rejected this offer too, just as she had rejected those that came before it and just as she rejected those that followed. Young men came and went, the years did not slow their pace, and Chaya Ita still didn't have a *chasan.*

As the years passed, the number of offers she received decreased. Suddenly, the distinguished Reb Shaul found himself chasing after the very same *shadchanim* who had once pursued him. "What about the son of . . . ? He's engaged? Really? And David from R.? He's younger than she is? I understand. What about Yosef, Moshe, Yerucham . . . ?"

It was clear to Reb Shaul that his daughter's age was not static. She was growing older. The two discussed the matter a number of times. "You're twenty-eight, Chaya Ita," Reb Shaul once told her. "Perhaps you should compromise.

Perhaps Gavriel S. suits you. After all, both of you are sitting and waiting. What will be? I won't live forever."

Chaya Ita listened and, as always, answered him quietly and politely. She was never rude to her parents. "Father, please understand that I can't marry someone who doesn't suit me."

"But how do you know he doesn't suit you?"

"It's a feeling. Something I know. I can't explain it. I just feel that way."

"But perhaps what you are looking for doesn't exist?"

"I know what you want to say. No, Father, I'm not searching for something that doesn't exist. I'm looking for a good *bachur* who will suit me."

"And were there no good *bachurim*?"

"Who suited me?"

"And how did you know that they didn't suit you?"

These arguments took place every week. Reb Shaul would make his points calmly, gently. He never hurt her feelings or lost his temper. However, he also never quite managed to conceal the pain in his voice.

Once Chaya Ita heard both parents discussing her. It was a conversation full of pain and sorrow. "*Ribbono shel Olam*," she heard her father sigh, "what will become of our dear daughter? Are we doomed to see her languish in our home until her hair turns white?"

When he said this, Chaya Ita felt a kind of shock. At the time, she didn't understand its significance, yet, years later, she realized that it was at that instant she had first understood that a problem did exist.

For a while, she decided to compromise. She suffered insulting offers in silence solely to put her parents' hearts at ease. But deep down, she knew she could not marry a man if even just meeting him was some kind of sacrifice.

৵ *Chapter Four: Loneliness*

The years continued to flow by. Chaya Ita turned thirty-two. The insulting offers became stinging ones. Chaya Ita saw how her father would wince whenever one *shadchan* or another was kind enough to dispose of his wares. When the offers became absolutely degrading, Chaya Ita suggested that Reb Shaul send the *shadchanim* away. But he argued. "And who will find you a *shidduch*? What good will it do me to bury my head in the sand?"

Soon enough, that worry, too, ceased to perturb Chaya Ita. The last of the *shadchanim* stopped showing their faces and making their voices heard in Reb Shaul's house. Only one was left with his absurd offers: Menash'ke.

The years were not kind to Chaya Ita. She was not as pretty as she had been in her youth, though traces of beauty still graced her face. She sat in her parents' home, unwanted.

Sometimes Menash'ke would drop by for a visit. Every now and then, he would remove from the depths of his pocket a crumpled list of names. Sometimes he would mumble something about a fine prospect he had heard about somewhere out west. The four of them knew that these were just empty words.

Those were sad days for Chaya Ita and her parents — indeed, for the whole family. She readily perceived her father's dejection every morning and her mother's quiet concern when their eyes would meet. There were no more arguments. She and her parents seemed to have an unspoken agreement that there was nothing more to argue about.

There were days on which Chaya Ita felt her heart was about to burst. Now she was prepared to make sweeping compromises. She was ready to make many sacrifices, if not for her own sake, then at least for the sake of her parents. Only now there was no one to accept her sacrifices.

She knew all too well that her friends' children were past bar mitzvah age. She knew that now she would be willing to marry most of the young men she had once rejected. Others, however, had preceded her. The hourglass of her youth was emptying its very last grains of sand. What should she do? What would become of her? There wasn't even anyone with whom she could share her sorrow.

Chaya Ita cried. She cried over the long days that had passed and over the difficult days that were yet to come.

"What will be? What will become of me?"

❧ Chapter Five: One Last Chance

One day, Menash'ke arrived. This time, he didn't inquire about anyone's health. He didn't exchange pleasantries. He just said, "This is it. I have found a *shidduch* for Chaya Ita."

Chaya Ita and her parents gathered around the large table and waited for Menash'ke to speak. They were excited. They knew that Menash'ke wasn't usually so direct, and they were therefore confident that this time he had something special to offer.

"Menachem Leiber," he said.

"Leiber? Menachem? Surely you don't mean the window-frame repairman!" exclaimed Reb Shaul.

"He is precisely the person I am speaking about. I just wonder why I never thought of him till today. He is the man for Chaya Ita. I have no doubt about it. He is of good character. He is serious. He —"

"But Menash'ke," Reb Shaul said, cutting him short. "You don't mean to offer my daughter an *am ha'aretz* who can't even analyze a *sugyah* properly?"

"He is capable of supporting his family. He's unusually generous, and he's also very nice-looking, don't you agree? He will be a loving and devoted husband, and her life with him will be good. You can find nothing wrong with him."

Silence. Chaya Ita retreated to the kitchen, and Reb Shaul tried politely to explain to Menash'ke why Menachem Leiber was not suitable for Chaya Ita.

"He is a wonderful person," Reb Shaul agreed, "and he'll make an excellent husband. I think he's among those who attend the *daf yomi shiur* in shul every day. But —" here he stopped short and fell into deep thought. Suddenly, he cried out, "You're right, Menash'ke. I can't find any real reason to oppose it. But please try to persuade Chaya Ita . . . "

The *shadchan* rushed to the kitchen and found a pale Chaya Ita. Menash'ke knew that added words would be futile. He knew that Chaya Ita was beyond any persuasion. It had to be something dramatic.

Menash'ke sat and began to describe an imaginary picture of the blissful, made-in-Heaven marriage of Chaya Ita and Menachem. He shut his eyes while he spoke, painting the future in rosy colors. He sat that way for a long time, and in the end, as if waking up from a reverie, he opened his eyes and saw a crooked smile on Chaya Ita's face — a smile he interpreted as a sneer.

With that, his patience snapped. He hurled the following remarks at her: "Listen carefully, young lady! A lot of choices you don't have. You must choose between marrying Menachem Leiber — which means a home, family, children and *nachas* — or loneliness, sorrow, terrifying silence, and hopelessness. That's the situation. Do you understand?"

Chaya Ita burst into tears.

"Stop, I beg of you," cried Reb Shaul, who had overheard.

Menash'ke rushed to the front door. "I'll stop," he said. "But know that this is your last chance, Chaya Ita. If I were in your place, I would agree to marry" — he paused to search for an appropriate word — "a blockhead. Do you understand? I would marry a blockhead rather than remain alone." The door slammed shut, and the weeping Chaya Ita fell into her father's arms.

The next morning, Reb Shaul told Menash'ke that he could proceed with the *shidduch*. Yes, his daughter had thought it over. She had cried all night, and in the morning had come to them red-eyed to announce her decision. She would agree to marry Menachem Leiber, if he'd agree to marry her. No, she didn't need a lot of meetings. One would be enough for her.

❧ Chapter Six: Menachem Leiber

When Menash'ke told Menachem Leiber that Chaya Ita had consented to consider his offer, he was over-whelmed. Suddenly he felt afraid. He, Menachem Leiber, the window-frame repairman, was about to enter such a family? He was to marry the great *yachsente*, Chaya Ita? The news was too good to be true.

Menachem Leiber was a simple *bachur*. Orphaned of his father at an early age, he had been forced to work as a hired hand. At first, he had taken all sorts of jobs. In time, he discovered that he had a talent for carpentry. He had apprenticed himself to an elderly window-frame repairman, and when the old man retired, Menachem had inherited the business. Within a few years, he was installing window frames for most of the new houses built in town. Sometimes he would be asked to repair or replace the window frames of older homes as well.

Menachem was a sturdy fellow. His face was handsome and sincere. He was a good man. Apparently his fellow townsmen had forgotten that he was still unmarried and had therefore made very few efforts to offer him a *shidduch*. Some attempts had been made but had been rejected straight-away. There were a number which had made some progress...and had then stopped. Menachem had reached the age of thirty-one. He was younger than Chaya Ita by four years.

They had one meeting. Chaya Ita asked him a number of questions, and he replied in his typically brief manner. Menachem didn't ask anything. He told Chaya Ita that he wanted to marry her, and that he saw it as a privilege to join the family. Menachem told Chaya Ita that he knew quite well the reasons she had agreed to consider marrying him. He knew he wasn't worthy but he promised her he would do his utmost to become worthy.

At the end of the meeting, Chaya Ita informed her parents that she would marry Menachem Leiber.

The three of them burst into tears.

ꙮ *Chapter Seven: Marriage*

It was a bittersweet wedding. Many thick-bearded men — Menachem's fellow workers — were present. They danced, even though they were unfamiliar with the art of dancing. They conversed in their own simple language. They clapped Reb Shaul on the shoulders instead of shaking his hand...and quite soon they grew tired and dozed off in their chairs. They were, after all, working men.

All of Chaya Ita's friends attended the *simchah*. The general consensus was, "What a waste. What a pity for the good years." On the other hand, they were happy that at long last Chaya Ita, whom all had expected to marry the greatest of the great, had at least made some kind of a match.

Menachem danced endlessly, filled with joy. He thanked Hashem for the *chesed* He had done by finding him so worthy a mate. It was the happiest day of his life.

Chaya Ita's happiness, though, was marred. Deep within her heart she felt that she had thrown away all her hopes and dreams. She saw her marriage as a great sacrifice she had made for her parents' sake. And perhaps, she thought, perhaps for her own sake as well.

At the end of the wedding, Menachem took Chaya Ita to their new home. Chaya Ita was excited and a bit frightened. She told this to Menachem but he only smiled his usual tranquil smile and said, "Like every bride, I suppose."

❧ Chapter Eight: Menachem and Chaya Ita

Their lives took on a routine, yet there was a tragic element to their marriage. Menachem thought the world of his wife, while Chaya Ita merely tolerated his presence, as if she were doing a rare act of kindness. In her heart, she tried to fight this feeling. It was difficult, though, for her to erase in one fell swoop her lifelong dream of marrying a refined, well-spoken, erudite Torah scholar.

Menachem was a far cry from a Torah scholar. True, he attended the *daf yomi shiur* on a regular basis but it was clear that even this basic course of study was as difficult for him as the Splitting of the Red Sea. Although Menachem was by nature a sensitive, refined person, he had never been taught the rules of proper etiquette. Thus, whenever the couple had to make a social call, Chaya Ita would drill him in how to act and, even more important, in how not to act. Menachem would listen quietly to her instructions and behave accordingly.

She never asked him about his studies in the *daf yomi shiur*, attaching no importance to them. She probably didn't know how he longed for her to ask such questions, how proud he was that he sacrificed his time to study Torah, and how disappointed he was by her indifference to his sacrifice.

They never discussed his work. Chaya Ita preferred to blot it out of her mind. It was as if his window-frame company did not exist, as if her husband had no hand in running it successfully. Menachem, with his keen senses, perceived how she felt. Sometimes he would slip and, out of habit, accidentally say, "Do you know, Chaya Ita, in whose house I —" But then he would remember and stop short. Silence would prevail, until Chaya Ita would raise another subject, as if nothing had happened.

There were days when a sudden melancholy would overcome Chaya Ita. She never shared her private feelings with Menachem. Yet he knew quite well why she was so unhappy. At such times, he would enter the house on tip-toe, as if trying to reduce his presence to the minimum.

There were tranquil times, too, in which a cheerful mood would suddenly overtake Chaya Ita. Menachem would then lose some of his shyness, and the two would sit and chat. Those were rare moments of mercy, which Menachem would bury deep in his heart and preserve for difficult hours. And there were many such hours.

Two years passed before Menachem and Chaya Ita were blessed with their first child, a son. The nine months preceding the birth were very difficult for both of them. Chaya Ita suffered from fluctuating moods. Menachem would soothe her, speaking calmly when she grumbled, but his heart would break.

One time he mustered the courage to say, "Do you know something, Chaya Ita? Both of us are human beings. We can give to each other, be happy together, appreciate one another. Do you know how much I admire you? Do you know that you could get so much happiness from your life, if you only wished?"

Chaya Ita's eyes filled with tears. She did not answer but thought to herself, *He doesn't understand. He will never understand, poor thing.* She pitied him with all her heart. And he, who sensed this, began to grasp how far reality was from his rosy dreams.

He decided to plunge himself into his work as a refuge from his thoughts. Quite rapidly, he expanded his business and opened a large woodworking shop, which specialized not only in window frames but in all types of carpentry. His business began to flourish, and he saw blessing in his labor.

As his workshop grew larger, he allowed himself to hire laborers. During the time thus freed, Menachem would involve himself in communal affairs. He took care of needy families, he helped widows and orphans and cared for the many elderly and homeless people of his town. He did all this quietly and modestly. No one but he knew a thing about his charitable activities, least of all his wife, Chaya Ita.

In time, Menachem became esteemed by all. Nearly everyone had been helped by him or knew someone he had helped.

Everyone loved Menachem. "A good *bachur*," people would call him. "A wonderful *bachur* . . ." Yes, even though he was over forty, they still called him a *bachur*.

Rabbis began to summon him. They entrusted him with weighty missions and secrets of communal importance. They appreciated his reliability and praised his selfless devotion to sacred endeavors, his good character traits, and genuine *yiras Shamayim*.

And yes, they also admired his simplicity, the same simplicity that had caused him so much sorrow in his private life. They envied his share in the World to Come.

Nearly everyone appreciated, admired and respected Menachem. Nearly everyone.

Ten years passed since the wedding of Menachem and Chaya Ita. They had five children, two boys and three girls. Chaya Ita assumed responsibility for their education and for molding the boys into *talmidei chachamim. If I don't, who will?* she thought.

As always, Menachem continued to treat her with respect. He still spoke to her gently, as he had ever since he had known her. He still bore with fortitude her outbursts — and her bad moods.

Only one person knew everything: Reb Shaul. He knew his daughter's emotional makeup and patterns of thought quite well, and that's why he admired and respected Menachem more than any of his other sons-in-law.

Reb Shaul's love for Menachem was deep and heartfelt. "My dear son-in-law," he would call him, and from the very tone of Reb Shaul's words, Menachem would sense what his father-in-law wanted to tell him but dared not.

ᔟ *Chapter Nine: The Accident*

It was a rainy winter's day. Menachem was perched on a windowsill at the top of the building where his company was doing carpentry work. With his strong left arm, he fastened the window frame into place. In his right arm he held a hammer and prepared to reinforce one of the nails he had previously inserted.

Something went wrong. Menachem swung his hammer in the direction of the frame with all his might, missed it, and, from the strength of the blow, was hurled to the bottom of the building.

A tremendous thud was heard. His workers rushed to see what had happened, and a shout burst forth from their mouths.

"M...e...n...a...ch...e...m!"

Bleeding and unconscious, Menachem was brought to the hospital. The doctors examined him and determined that he had been fatally injured and that his hours were numbered.

At that time, Chaya Ita was sitting in her garden, watching her youngest daughter take her very first steps. Something the child had done amused her, and she burst into peals of laughter. She felt good.

Suddenly she heard a noise. A few people dressed like workmen seemed to be looking for someone. Inexplicably, they turned to her. "Are you the wife of Menachem Leiber?"

"Yes. What happened?"

The man hesitated. "There was an accident."

"What happened? Tell me! Don't hide anything from me."

"He . . . fell from the building."

Chaya Ita let out a cry of anguish. "What happened to him? Tell me! Don't torture me!"

"He's injured. His condition is not good. We had better hurry."

They rushed to the hospital. When they arrived, Chaya Ita noticed the looks directed at her. The looks said, "There's no hope."

"Let me in to see him," wailed Chaya Ita. "Let me go in."

She was ushered into the room in which her injured husband lay. A tremor passed through her body. "Take leave of him. He hasn't much longer to live," said the doctor as he closed the door and left.

Chaya Ita was terror-stricken. "Menachem is about to die," she murmured. "It can't be. Menachem can't die."

She felt as if her world had been destroyed. She looked at the sturdy man who lay on the bed wounded and barely breathing.

"No-o-o-o!" she screamed.

She heard herself speaking to him. "You can't die, Menachem. Listen, I'm your wife, Chaya Ita. You must live, Menachem, do you hear?"

Memories of the times when he had soothed, comforted and showered her with compliments flooded her mind. Suddenly, it was as if his inner world opened up before her. Suddenly, she knew that all those years she had lived with a pure, noble-spirited man of unusual character.

She was too late. Ten years too late. Only now did she realize that her husband, Menachem, was the best and most remarkable person she had ever known. Why hadn't she realized this before? How had she been so blind as to not appreciate his lofty traits? She knew now that she had merited a husband who was unique among men, a husband she was about to lose in a matter of moments.

I've always been too late, she thought to herself. *I've always understood things only after they happen. My life is one long saga of suffering which I brought upon myself. What will become of me? What will be?*

Through her tears, she heard herself pleading, "Don't die, Menachem. Don't die. Only now do I realize that I am not worthy of being the dust under your feet. If only you knew how I long to tell you all this."

Her voice grew hysterical. "Give me a chance, Menachem," she sobbed. "Give me one chance. I'll make it up to you for all those years. Feel my pain and know that I think the world of you. Forgive me for all those years — even though I don't deserve to ever be forgiven."

She burst into unrestrained weeping, the tormented weeping of one who has nothing left.

Suddenly she noticed that she wasn't alone in the room. Her father was with her. His eyes were closed, and warm tears wet his white beard.

Reb Shaul clasped his daughter and said nothing. Silently, he wept.

The two heard a sound. They looked at the helpless man who lay on the bed. He was trying to say something but found speaking difficult.

They moved closer to him, frightened and anxious. Chaya Ita bent close to her injured husband's face and heard him whisper in her ear, "I heard you... Chaya Ita... I heard you... You have restored my soul... My injury... is a kindness... from Above...

"It is still... not too late," he added heavily. "Hashem... will give... us... the... strength... "

"Chaya Ita... we'll begin... anew."

From
the
Beginning

The news that Reb Yosef had become a first-grade rebbe caused quite a stir in town.

"Yosef? A first-grade rebbe?" people wondered. "Couldn't he have found a more important position?"

It was the first day in Elul. Summer refused to make way for fall. The sunbeam which penetrated Reb Yosef's classroom from the other side of the window made its way through the rows of first-graders whose first day it was in *cheder*, and landed on his forehead.

It would be a mistake, though, to think that the sweat on Reb Yosef's brow was caused by the sunbeam. It was his heart sending signals of distress which threatened to burn his soul. Leaning on the desk, he recalled the words of his best friend, Gershon.

"Consider what you're about to do," Gershon had told him. "Think about the fact that instead of using your mind and the unique organizational talents you have for matters of the utmost importance, you'll be wasting them trying to explain to children why the Torah begins with the letter *beis* and teaching them how to write it. You'll be busy trying to go down to the level of their childish minds in order to find a way to explain to them the meaning of the word *'bereshis.'* "

Yet here he was, standing in front of those same first-graders, some of whom were wailing and wanted to run away. Rashi's words — "an infant runs away from school" — flashed through his mind, and the doubts which gnawed at his heart nearly overwhelmed him. At that moment, he, Yosef, was afraid of dashing the hopes of those who had expected so much of him. The word "infant" seemed to point to the fate which awaited him, to the disappointing future he was carving out for himself.

The wailing of the children grew louder. *I'll think about it later*, he mused, as he held his *Chumash*. *The children are waiting for me*, he thought, and remembered that it was that very phrase which had caused him to accept the *cheder* principal's offer of a job. "The children are waiting for you," the principal had said when he noticed Yosef speaking to a few three year olds who were running wild in the hallway of the shul and disrupting prayers. "The children are waiting for you," he had repeated, pointing to the children who looked at Yosef adoringly, as if anticipating his forgiveness.

Now here he was — facing thirty children! What should he do next?

He forced his biggest smile. "Children! Let's all cry together. One, two, three...," he said in a mournful tone, which wasn't forced at all.

All of a sudden, he noticed that he was the only one crying. The children had stopped their crying and were looking at him in surprise.

He knew that the time had come. "I see that you don't want to cry," he said. "Never mind. Open your beautiful *Chumashim,* and let us begin from the beginning — from *Bereshis.*"

Within a month, every schoolchild in town knew who the best rebbe was. Within two months, all of the city's principals, all of the various supervisors, and all of the parents who were trying to decide where to register their children for the forthcoming year knew, too.

Reb Yosef taught the children why the Torah begins with the letter *beis.* He found, after a lot of soul-searching, the way to convey the meaning of the word *"bereshis"* to the tender minds of the children. He found the courage to play with the children in the sand, to slide down the slide with them, and to speak their language.

He led them through what at first had appeared to them as a maze of letters and dots, and they followed him, hanging on to his coattails and, in a manner known only to them, to his heart as well.

Fall vanquished summer and was soon conquered by winter. The sand in the schoolyard became filled with puddles, and the resulting mess found its way to his washing machine at home. At first, he would try to hide it, attempting to clean the sand and mud stains before his wife saw them. But he caught himself and realized that he was still ashamed of his occupation, that he had not yet made peace with it despite loving it with his whole heart.

His wife, an *eshes chayil,* was rather pleased with his new occupation and complimented him on his success. But he attributed this to her good, tolerant nature. He took her words for encouragement, and the need to encourage only proved to him that in her eyes, and the eyes of many others as well, his status had been lowered, and that was why he needed encouragement.

He loved his work and was ashamed of that love. *Okay, so I've failed in the race to fulfill my potential,* he would muse. *But to love what I am doing?*

Summer arrived once more and dried up the puddles left by winter. The sunbeam which danced on the side of Reb Yosef's desk reminded him that it was nearly Elul. When it would land in the middle of his face, he knew, a new group of crying children would be sitting before him. Would he cry along with them this time, too? Would he stay in his job — or leave it?

When the sunbeam reached the center of his desk, it found him there again. Vacation had filled him with longing for the little children, for *Bereshis*. He was ashamed of these feelings, remembering what people always told him: "What a waste of talent. What a waste."

The years fluttered by like the sunbeam which visited him regularly each year, like the children who were already grown and filled yeshivah benches. Many of them would occasionally pass by the *cheder* in which he taught, enter the yard where he was sliding down the slide with one or another of the children, and he, embarrassed, would have to brush off the sand which clung to his clothes to ask them about their studies, the *sugyah* they were learning, sometimes feeling stabs of jealousy as he watched them rush back to their yeshivos with their beloved Gemaras under their arms, while he was always forced to return, to continue to begin from *Bereshis.*

Reb Yosef taught first-graders for fifteen years. Everyone had nothing but praise for him: "The best rebbe in town"; "He's put all of his talents into the children."

They were pleased with him. Yet he, only he, wasn't pleased with himself.

One day the members of his shul asked him to coordinate the construction of the new building they were planning. Reb Yosef was chosen for the job over all others because everyone knew of his inherent talents, his expertise, and his unusual organizational skills.

He supervised the construction in the best possible manner. He hired the quickest and most skilled workmen, purchased the most suitable building materials, and, within a year's time, a beautiful shul was ready for use.

It was Mordechai the building contractor, one of the shul's members, who was so impressed by Reb Yosef's skills that he offered him a partnership in his construction firm.

Mordechai had no sons. "I am too old to manage my firm alone. It's a shame for your talents to be wasted. Join me and you won't have to worry about making a living for the rest of your life."

At first, Reb Yosef refused. However, Mordechai's words slowly penetrated his mind. "I'm a wasted talent anyway. Why shouldn't my family at least benefit from my wasted talents?"

When Reb Yosef's partnership in Mordechai's firm became known, opinions were divided.

There were those who said, "At long last Reb Yosef is making the most of his real talent instead of burying it in the sandbox!"

There were, however, a few who said, "If he isn't teaching, he should have at least stayed in the Torah world. He could have become a *rosh mesivta* or a *rosh yeshivah*. He's capable of that, too, isn't he?"

Reb Yosef was as successful with the sand and cement trucks, with the workers who built the numerous buildings he planned, as he had been with the children and the sandbox. He became wealthy and was given great honor for his large donations to charity. He reasoned that at long last he had received confirmation that he was not a wasted talent.

Nevertheless, when he would remember the children, the sunbeam left all alone — surely angry at his desertion and surprised by his failure to appear at their yearly rendezvous — when he would remember the *sefer Bereshis* which he had begun anew year after year, something would pinch his heart.

Reb Yosef remained in the building business for another fifteen years. In the meantime, Mordechai's strength had waned, and he sold his share of the business to Reb Yosef, who, with this investment, became the wealthiest man in town. Yet still, deep down, Reb Yosef knew he was not satisfied.

Suddenly, days of hardship came. The building business hit an unprecedented slump. Reb Yosef was left with skeletons of buildings and no buyers. His bank account began to dwindle, and many buyers found themselves left with only the paper promises of a building in which they had invested all their hopes — and all their money.

An accountant advised him to declare bankruptcy, but a man like Reb Yosef would not allow himself to take such a step. Slowly, he sold all of the property he still owned and came to terms with his creditors; he sold his unfinished buildings, along with their lots, to other contracting firms and managed to complete the apartments of each and every one of the buyers.

And as for himself? He was left stripped of all his assets.

All of them!

It was the last days in Av. A solitary, dejected-looking man roamed the city's streets, his thoughts scattered, his gaze unfocused, his heart shooting arrows at the fibers of his soul.

His hair had grown white; his eyes were sunken. Sorrow was the only feeling his image conveyed.

He went wherever his feet carried him, until he stopped opposite a building in whose entrance stood a young man who called his name.

"Reb Yosef!"

"Who are you?" he asked despondently.

"Shlomo Goldstein. Don't you remember? You taught me in your first class, thirty years ago."

"And what are you doing here?" he asked when he realized that he was standing in front of the *cheder* in which he used to teach.

"I am," the man replied in an embarrassed tone, "the principal of this *cheder*. Would you believe it?"

"Wonderful," Reb Yosef replied in a voice as distracted as his gaze.

"What are you doing nowadays?" the principal asked him.

"Nothing!"

"Nothing?"

Both were silent.

"Wait a minute. You've come at exactly the right time. School will begin in two days, and I still don't have a first-grade rebbe. Your coming was Heaven-sent."

"Me? A first-grade rebbe?"

"Reb Yosef, don't you know that we have never forgotten you? Don't you know that every rebbe who has taught here during the past fifteen years was measured against you? Don't you know...?"

"Don't I know what?"

"How much... I loved you."

It was the first day of Elul. Summer refused to make way for fall. The sunbeam which penetrated Reb Yosef's classroom from the other side of the window made its way through the rows of first-graders whose first day it was in *cheder* and landed on Reb Yosef's forehead.

The sound of crying filled the classroom but this time, Reb Yosef didn't hear it. His head was buried in his hands, and his body shook with sobs.

The children stopped crying, and several of them hesitantly approached his desk on the other side of the sunbeam.

One of them tugged Reb Yosef's coattails. "Rebbe, don't cry. We stopped already."

Then Reb Yosef rose with determination, a smile on his face. This time, it was not forced. "Sit down children," he said. They obeyed.

His hands held a *Chumash*, and he opened to... begin from the beginning, from *Bereshis*.

The Old House
in the
Village

Somewhere on Beit Kamah, a moshav beside the famous crossroads in the highway that transverses the valley, stands a plain, old house. It has weathered many years, and no man knows the stormy saga hidden within. Only a small sign several hundred feet away on which is written, "The Ancient Cemetery," alludes to something — but even it cannot begin to tell the full story.

❧ Nat Zimmerman

When Reb Moshe Zimmerman died at a ripe old age, his seven children huddled together in his small house in Beit Kamah to sit shiva. There were five sons and two daughters, all married and with children, except for one of them, Netanel Zimmerman, who was still unmarried.

This wasn't the only difference between them. While most of Reb Moshe's other children had followed in his path, keeping the mitzvos and even doing a bit more here and there, Netanel, who for some reason was called Nat, did not act like that at all. Actually, Nat Zimmerman was considered a glatt kosher *chiloni* — a secular Jew — and many said that Nat distanced himself from mitzvos with the very same fervor that his siblings observed them.

Nat had caused his mother, Bella, who had died a decade earlier, as well as his father, who had died that week, a great deal of anguish. His brothers though, made no mention of that fact, especially since they were very grateful to Nat for the devoted care he had given to their parents while they were still alive, such as, for instance, making sure to live with them in the old house on the moshav until their final days.

Actually, Shmuel, the oldest of the brothers, who was himself a grandfather of two, felt that the honor and respect Netanel had shown for their parents had been exceptional, and that he would surely be richly rewarded for it from Above. But when he would mention this to Netanel, Nat's expression would darken, and he would give such a sharp retort to his brother's remarks that the faces of all his other brothers and sisters would turn red.

They never even came close to fighting, though. No matter what their conflicts and differences of opinion, the children of Reb Moshe Zimmerman never fought. And there were as many conflicts and differences of opinion as there were white hairs in the beard of Shmuel, the eldest.

Truth be told, over the years Nat did everything in his power to magnify the differences of opinion and to strike up some kind of argument with his brothers, but he never managed to achieve his aim. Any time he tried to make a verbal attack, or even half a verbal attack, on his brother's beliefs, they would remind him of the wonderful mitzvos he did for their parents, even adding all sorts of complimentary remarks, and in the end, Nat would come out of it quite pleased. He had managed to shoot verbal darts at his brothers and receive a bouquet of praises from them at the very same time.

Even during those sad shiva days, Nat was deluged with compliments — probably because he gave them an equal, if not greater, share of criticism.

Nat's brothers felt that in addition to the sorrow he felt over the death of his beloved father, he was undergoing a depression laced with fear and uncertainty. He spoke a lot about the future, about "what will be" and "what will happen to me," but his brothers couldn't understand his fears. Had their father helped him in any way? The opposite was true. During his last few years Reb Moshe had been totally dependent on Nat, something which had tied him down a lot recently. Of course, the loss of a beloved father is painful; but what was the nature of such a depression? What was so terrifying about the future?

Actually, Nat didn't understand his fears either. Had he looked into his heart, though, he would have realized that he feared the impending separation from his brothers and sisters, from his entire family. He knew that now, after his father's death, they would no longer visit the small house on Shabbos and holidays, and, subconsciously, strains of distress were woven into the loneliness.

Nat knew all too well how happy those visits of his brothers and sisters and their children made him. They were the only moments of joy to break the monotony of his loneliness. And Nat was a very lonely man — a man without a wife, without children, and even without friends.

The days of sitting shiva ended, the brothers packed their belongings, and Nat stood on the threshold of his house and looked at them, not understanding the heavy feeling in his heart. There is no moment sadder than that moment of Nat's as he stood there watching his brothers and sisters leave the small house on the moshav, perhaps for the last time in their lives.

And then he remembered something which had completely slipped his mind, and he called out, "Wait a minute! Our father left a will, and I think that this is the right time to read it to everyone. Don't you agree?"

They put down their bags and went back inside. They waited while Nat went up to the attic, where they had always hidden as children and where the will of their father, Reb Moshe, had been placed.

After several minutes, he came down, covered with dust, and opened a large, brown envelope from which he pulled out a single page with the heading, written in a trembling hand: "My last will and testament."

And this is what Reb Moshe Zimmerman had written: "Since I have no possessions other than my house and the land surrounding it, I hereby bequeath my house to all my seven children equally, on the condition that it will never be sold. My dearly beloved son, Netanel, will be in charge of the house and will live in it the rest of his life. I have one request from my other children: that they visit the house together with their families once a year, for the entire week of Pesach, and that they do this for the rest of their lives. If they abide by my wishes, they will receive abundant blessings from Heaven."

In the remainder of the will, Reb Moshe divided a number of personal items among his children, such as a watch, an antique painting and a tallis. To Netanel, he bequeathed the contents of the house, so that he would be able to live comfortably and prepare for the guests who would visit him every year.

In truth, Reb Moshe's children were surprised by the will and took their leave of Nat without looking him in the face. In their opinion, their father, may he rest in peace, had asked too much of Netanel. Fearing that deep down Nat was sorry they even existed, they left quickly, one by one.

As soon as they had gone, Nat rushed to his room, sat down on his bed and burst into bitter tears over the death of his father, to whom he had been so close, and over his own life and what would be left of it from now on.

If Nat would have probed a bit deeper, he would have discovered that those tears were actually tears of relief — relief from his dread that he would never again see his family, the only people in the world who ever gave him any attention, warmth and love.

Nat sat and awaited the arrival of Pesach which would bring his family back to him and save him from his loneliness. However, there were many months until Pesach, and Nat, who until then had been busy taking care of his father, was left facing four walls (actually, more) and a beautiful, well-tended garden which, although it needed two hours of care daily, still left him with many hours — too many hours — in which he had nothing to do.

❧ Loneliness

Loneliness entered Nat's life, which wasn't at all difficult for it to. It had always been a guest of honor there, for Nat had no wife or children to relieve his loneliness and bring some happiness into his life. Nat sat there alone and forsaken, not knowing which was worse — the long day, which stretched on endlessly, with the rays of the sun beating down from dawn to dusk, or the dark night, long and cold, which at best brought with it sad, frightening dreams, and at the worst, a never-ending struggle with insomnia.

On the one hand, there was nothing more heart-breaking for Nat than the long hours of the night when he would toss and turn in bed, close his eyes tightly and wait for sleep's salvation. On the other hand, those long and boring days with no beginning and no end took their toll. And he, a man in his forties, could not decide if the night was worse than the day, or the opposite; and in the end, he called it a draw.

One morning Nat was looking through the newspaper, and noticed on one of its inside pages that not far from the moshav some fellows called archaeologists were digging, with the goal of discovering artifacts from various eras. Nat had never shown any interest in excavations of any kind, except for the diggings he had made in the yard to put in fence posts. Then his eyes caught sight of a photo which showed the faces of several people dressed in long black coats just like those his brothers wore, and maybe even longer.

According to the caption, those same people were trying to disrupt and even halt the excavations, claiming that there was an ancient cemetery located in exactly the same area, where people who had lived hundreds of years ago, or perhaps even longer, lay buried. The writer did not bother to commend those same figures — the opposite.

Without saying a word, Nat rose, ambled over to the old tractor parked at the end of his yard, and headed for the excavation site. When he reached it, he encountered men digging, surrounded by dozens of men dressed in black. Then and there, Nat decided that the time had come for him to take action.

He began to argue vehemently with those "men in black." He shouted and accused, while they tried to explain, but to no avail. Nat was actually only quoting what he had read in the paper, but as the argument escalated, he became more and more convinced that what he was saying was right. "Who are you to interfere with progress?" he roared at them. "Let the scientists do their work," he shouted heatedly.

Soon, some of the archaeologists approached him and treated him like a comrade. They invited him into their tents during their coffee break, and before they even asked who or what, he began to spout his philosophy and explain that he had always supported excavations like theirs and others, and that he had always opposed cemeteries of all sorts. When he saw that they enjoyed his remarks, he embellished them here and there. He hadn't felt so good in a long time.

Had Nat looked around him, his eyes would have met those of a young man who wrote down everything he said on a small note pad. But Nat was too impassioned by his own words to notice anything.

After that, Nat once more confronted the "men in black," hurling scorn and derision at them, and even trying to shove them aside with his strong arms. An actual fistfight would have developed had not the leader of the black-hatters, Rabbi Spiegel, intervened, preventing his followers from giving Nat what was coming to him. Rabbi Spiegel had to make a special effort to calm one of the black-hatted demonstrators, the youngest of the group, who was, by nature, more impassioned than the rest and who, with eyes aflame, was all too ready to respond to Nat's pushes. Rabbi Spiegel dragged him away, saying, "He's older than you are," but for Nat that wasn't enough. He turned to one of the policemen who was there and complained that the young man had attacked him. And what did the policemen do if not pull the young man into a paddy wagon and speed away?

Nat did not notice another young person, equipped with a camera, who documented the entire incident.

Night fell. The archaeologists completed their work, and the policemen allowed the black-hatted men to go down into the excavation site and gather the bones which had been unearthed there. Nat continued to stand there, heaping them with abuse, until they had completed their work and left the site.

Only then did Nat allow himself to return home to discover that the day had passed and was no more. He rode back on his old tractor to the dark and lonely house. Once again, feelings of sadness and loneliness engulfed him. Nat found himself waiting for the morning, which promised at least some sort of activity.

The next morning, when Nat opened the morning paper, as was his wont, what did he see on its front page if not a picture of himself, struggling with the demonstrators? And what was the caption if not: "Ultra-Orthodox demonstrators who tried to attack Nat Zimmerman, a member of Moshav Beit Kamah, were pushed back by police. One of them, Shimon Domb, was arrested and imprisoned for three days."

At that moment, Nat knew that a new dimension had been added to his life.

✷ Champion of Progress

From that day on, Nat wandered from excavation to excavation, from one stormy demonstration to another even stormier one. Nat turned out to be a man unafraid of battle and with a nose of stone. His picture was plastered all over the major newspapers, which were filled with full-page interviews with him. The telephone in his home didn't stop ringing. Nat became a celebrity in great demand.

Especially well known was his personal animosity toward Shimon Domb, the demonstrator who grappled with him constantly and was arrested time and time again.

After that first demonstration, Domb had shouted at him, "If you're so fair and decent, why didn't you say that you were the one who attacked me?"

Nat had snapped back, "I'm defending science. You want to return us to the Middle Ages."

"What's wrong with that?" retorted Domb, and the argument once more grew heated, nearly erupting into a fistfight. Once again, Domb was arrested, and again the two met at subsequent demonstrations.

One night, after a particularly stormy protest, and after Nat had again given interviews to various reporters and newscasters, the telephone rang. Nat lifted the receiver, and who was on the other end of the line if not his brother, Shmuel?

"*Shalom Alechem*, Netanel," said Shmuel. "How do you feel?"

Nat decided not to stay on the receiving end. "You won't be able to convince me. Nothing will help, so don't try to play on my heartstrings. True, we're brothers but that doesn't mean that —"

"Netanel," Shmuel replied, "I don't know what you're talking about."

"You don't know? There was nothing in your newspapers about the attack made on those who supported the archaeologists?"

"Sure there was, but what's the connection?" Shmuel asked with curiosity.

That's when Nat understood that Shmuel had not the slightest idea about his activities of the past week, and for some reason, he didn't have the courage to tell him.

"Then why are you calling?" he asked.

"First of all, to find out how you are," said Shmuel. "But aside from that," he continued hesitantly, "I called about Pesach, which is right around the corner. You know... the will... "

Nat was dumbfounded. Joy filled his heart. At long last, Pesach, which would fill the house with people and children, was drawing near — and he hadn't even begun to prepare for it! He started to think about how he could find room for everyone, how to invite them all and how to bring them, when suddenly he heard himself asking, "Are you prepared to stay in the home of someone like me, the head of those fighting against members of the Sacred Sites organization?

"Who is the head of — what are you talking about?" asked Shmuel.

"I'm the *moshavnik* farmer written about in your paper," said Nat. "You don't read secular papers, so you didn't see my picture." Nat took courage from what he had already said and added, "Because of me, those people went to jail. Now do you still want to come to me?"

A few moments of silence passed, and then Nat heard Shmuel say gently, "Is everything okay with you, Netanel?"

"Everything's fine," Nat replied.

"Then we'll come for Pesach, if you'll have us."

"And what about —"

"What interests me is that everything should be kosher. I trust you, Netanel. We'll bring the food and drink; you worry about places to sleep and cleaning the house. If you want I'll send a few of my children to come and kasher the kitchen. No, Netanel. I'm not impressed by what you just told me. I know you quite well and don't judge you unfavorably."

The conversation ended with Nat agreeing. Afterwards, he found himself wondering about his brother's final words.

During the days preceding Pesach, Nat prepared the rooms for his family, not neglecting, though, his demonstrations and his sharp opposition to those *charedim* who were "standing in the way of progress," as he put it.

At the last demonstration before Pesach, when Shimon Domb was, thanks to Nat's efforts, arrested for the umpteenth time, Domb shouted, as he was being dragged away by the police, "Just wait, Zimmerman. You think there's no justice and no judge? I've already pressed charges against you in court for attacking me. There are pictures. You —"

The door of the van closed, and a pale Nat remained rooted to the spot.

Pesach arrived, and with it, forty-three family members — Nat's six brothers and sisters and their spouses plus thirty-one children. The house was filled with the happy sounds of children playing. If, in the first minutes, Nat had tried to maintain some semblance of order, this semblance had been demolished without notice when the children began climbing on him and dragging him with them to the tractor for the traditional ride around the farm he always gave them when his father was still alive. And there was no happier person in the world than Nat struggling with the dozens of children who tried to take the wheel of the old contraption called a tractor away from him. He yelled at them, and they climbed on top of him, blowing the tractor's horn, which, judging by the loud honk it made, was the only part which hadn't aged.

Nat's encounter with his brothers was a lot cooler. Reports of his activities had reached their ears one way or another, and even though they had decided not to say a word or even half a word about the matter, it was difficult for them to hide their pain. But the children managed to thaw even this chill, and not more than an hour had passed after the last brother had finished unpacking his suitcases in the room given to him and his family for the week, when the brothers were already out touring the extensive grounds around the house, expressing their amazement over how much effort their brother had put into maintaining it.

Seder night arrived. Nat sat as usual and participated in all the customs. He enjoyed the evening very much, especially since he could not discern the slightest trace of criticism in his brother's remarks, criticism which he had expected to hear and had planned on refuting with his own cutting words.

The seven days flew by. Nat did not leave the house, even though he knew about several excavations being conducted not too far away. He weighed the pros and cons and decided to stay at home.

When the hour of parting arrived, he once again stood at the threshold of his house with the feelings familiar to him from the seven days of shiva and knew that, come what may, he would always look forward to Pesach.

ᴥ From Struggle to War

Two weeks after Pesach, two policemen knocked on Nat's door. They asked him to accompany them to the police station for questioning. Nat was shocked and offended to the depths of his being. Seeing that he had no choice but obey, he went with them.

When he arrived at the local police station, he was taken into a room for questioning. A young policeman showed him the testimony he had given the previous month about the attack by Shimon Domb — testimony which had led to Domb's arrest and three-day-long imprisonment. He confirmed that the testimony was indeed his, and then the policeman whipped out a packet of photographs in which Nat was seen pushing Rabbi Spiegel and Shimon Domb, who had come to Rabbi Spiegel's aid. The following pictures were close-ups of Rabbi Spiegel, showing scratches and bruises on his face, which even Nat found it hard to believe he was responsible for.

"Do you admit your guilt?" he heard the stern voice of the police officer ask.

"I didn't hear what you said," Nat quickly replied.

The officer read the charges against him, and Nat, who didn't know what to answer, heard himself saying the sentence declared by all criminals: "I want to consult a lawyer."

Reports of Nat's arrest appeared in all the papers. "Civil Rights Fighter Arrested For Bringing False Charges," screamed the headlines, and Nat, who was totally unprepared for such publicity, became depressed.

He was released on bail by his brothers, who rushed to his aid. They waited for him outside the jail and tried to find out how he was. But he refused to answer them and ordered a taxi to take him home. They followed him but when he got home, he locked the door and refused to respond to their knocks.

He spent a difficult night. When morning came, Nat awoke determined to intensify his battle despite the impending trial. In his mailbox was a note from his brothers, who had written, "You are still our brother." He tore the letter to shreds.

From that day on, Nat fought even harder. He recruited a number of members from his moshav and those of several nearby settlements and formed a group called "The Guardians of Science." The group's explicit goal was to fight against all those who would undermine the efforts of the archaeologists, claiming that they desecrated graves.

In addition to his general war, everyone knew that Nat had a personal war against Shimon Domb. Obsessively, he began to gather as much information about him as possible. He soon discovered that Shimon was an only child and that despite having reached the age of thirty, was still unmarried.

They would stand facing each other at every demonstration. Nat would insult Shimon, and Shimon would reply sweetly, quoting verses from Scripture and offering explanations. Nat never managed to disturb

Shimon's infuriating equanimity, except once, when he discovered how to get to him. It was when he said, "You're thirty, aren't you? By that age all your friends have eight children, and you're not even married! Anyway, who would want to marry someone like you!"

This was the first time that Shimon's face turned crimson, and Nat realized that he had gotten to him. From then on, he would remind Shimon of his unmarried state at every opportunity. A month passed before Shimon decided to answer him and quietly told Nat, "I'm thirty but you seem to be about fifty, so don't project your troubles on me."

Nat found himself declaring, "I'm not fifty! I'm only forty-six and two months," and as he said this, he understood how hurtful and cutting his words had been.

From then on, there was an unspoken agreement between them — about one subject only. They never, ever again tried to hurt each other about their still being unmarried.

❧ Shimon Domb

Shimon Domb was seventeen years old when his father, Simchah, had died. Until that time, Shimon was considered just about the most normal child there ever could be — one of those you'd never give a passing glance to even if he'd wave a red flag right in front of you. A regular, ordinary child.

He graduated from Talmud Torah, entered *yeshivah ketanah*, and continued on to *yeshivah gedolah*. His teachers and rebbes never complained about him; on the other hand, they also never went out of their way to commend him. That summed up Shimon Domb.

But from the day his father died, something seemed to break inside him. Because he was introverted, he very rarely shared his thoughts with his friends. Instead, he found the strangest ways to forget his grief.

Without anyone's noticing, Shimon started attending the demonstrations held by the Sacred Sites organization. Actually, even the volunteers of this organization wouldn't have paid any attention to him unless they had needed him for their activities. But in time, Shimon proved to be quite an effective organizer of successful demonstrations, and the organization's volunteers gradually began to include the youth in their plans and decision-making.

Shimon did not know that the head of the organization, Rabbi Spiegel, had spoken with his *rosh yeshivah* about him. The *rosh yeshivah* had been surprised to learn about Shimon's "extracurricular" activities but after several conversations, the two concluded that such activity was actually the best outlet for Shimon — not to mention the vital contribution he would be making to the organization.

In time, Shimon became a central figure in the organization, and all those in the field — archaeologists, policemen, demonstrators, and onlookers — got used to seeing Shimon as a permanent and essential fixture at every excavation, or every attempt at one.

So active was he that more than once members of the police force asked themselves how he could be at five events at the same time while they themselves hardly managed to get to two. But to this question, they never received an answer.

Years passed. Volunteers in the organization came and went, volunteered and changed — only Shimon remained permanently. He was as attached to Rabbi Spiegel as were the archaeologists attached to Jewish bones, and actually a lot more than that, because thanks to this closeness, a lot of archaeologists were prevented from becoming too attached to Jewish bones.

Over the years an unusual dependency developed between Shimon and Rabbi Spiegel. But the last ones to be aware of it were the two themselves, for they were too involved in their activities to find the time to dwell on such psychology, or any other.

Shimon's widowed mother did not say a word about her son's activities, until he reached marriageable age and passed it with no wedding in sight. At first she would make vague comments about the *nachas* she was waiting for. Then she increased the pressure, until Shimon got the message that there was something his mother wanted.

When he started to look for a *shidduch*, though, it became clear that most people tend to look at the cover and not at what's inside the book — and from whatever angle one looked at Shimon, the cover simply wasn't one of the most impressive. Take his clothes, for instance. Most of them showed signs of his having been dragged across the ground, thanks to the policemen and archaeologists. Aside from that, it was disturbing that Shimon wasn't glued to the benches of the yeshivah. It didn't add a single ounce of distinction, and there were those who said it added even less.

The fact that Shimon was frequently arrested by the police also didn't do much to increase the offers of marriage. That's because the number of girls willing to marry someone who comes and goes in jail is no larger than the number of those who are themselves willing to enter that same institution — which left Shimon with only the slimmest chances of finding a girl like that, or any other.

Only his mother and Rabbi Spiegel truly appreciated Shimon — because they took the trouble to open the book and look inside. And what they saw there was a pure and golden heart, excellent character, and an unusual concern and caring, not often found, for the well-being of others.

They also knew that Shimon was not only active on behalf of the bones of the dead but that he also gave generously of his time to those still alive. He could spend an entire Shabbos in a hospital beside the bed of an elderly patient, or run at the height of a family celebration to where many people lay injured to help the paramedics care for the wounded, and then afterwards stay to remove the dead bodies, even though this was far less enjoyable than dancing at any wedding.

There were infrequent moments when Shimon would pause and reflect on his life, and when he did so, he felt a pang of sadness. At those moments it wasn't pity for himself he felt, but rather for his widowed mother who didn't have the satisfaction of seeing her son married, with a family. Every once in a while, he thought about himself...

Then he would cry. He didn't like to cry at all, so he would quickly throw himself into some sort of activity to escape the painful reality of his situation.

Out of concern for his mother, he tried to persuade her to remarry. "It's not good to be alone," he would tell her. "It's time for you to find yourself a partner and put an end to living alone."

But his mother refused to hear of it. "Are you the one to tell me? What will be with you?" she would reply. "I've decided not to remarry until you find your partner in life."

Before you could turn around, Shimon had turned thirty, thus conquering hundreds if not thousands of *shadchanim* who had tried, along with his mother, to interest him in that business called "marriage."

Seder night of that same year, Shimon sat at the head of the table where the entire crowd of diners consisted of only one — his mother. That year, no one had taken the trouble to invite them, and that is why Shimon was softly reciting the Haggadah and looking at his mother, who hid her face in her hands. And if anyone would have peeked in at this scene, there's no doubt he would have seen the saddest Seder in the world.

At that very moment, what was Nat Zimmerman doing if not bargaining with his nieces and nephews over a certain piece of matzah called the *afikomen*.

Naturally, it was a lot of fun, and Nat entered, as he did every year, a world of complete happiness — a world he never knew during the other days of the year but only on the seven days of Pesach.

Nat gazed at his huge Seder table, flanked by scores of family members who filled his heart with joy and made his life worthwhile. The children's bright laughter once more resounded throughout the moshav, and Nat knew that those were the happiest days of his life.

Nat was prepared to give all the money in the world in order to keep those children — or at least some of them — with him all year round. Sometimes he thought he would even be willing to dress and act like his brothers, like what they call a *"ba'al teshuvah,"* if only to be happy like them, and if only to fill his world more than it was now. Nat knew that such a return was a small sacrifice compared with what he would be willing to give to be happy. That's why he was a little bit ashamed of himself for his vacillations and decided not to consider such possibilities again.

Yet Nat never hid from his brothers how important the annual visit was for him, and in a way, the contradiction sometimes perplexed him.

One such time occurred about a month before Pesach. Nat had asked some builders to expand the small house by adding two rooms. His few friends on the moshav asked him in surprise, "Why does a bachelor like you need such a large house?"

To which he replied with equal surprise, "Don't you know that on Pesach forty-three people are coming here?"

"You probably mean those same people who Pesach after Pesach turn your green lawn black," they teased.

Nat, confused, couldn't find the words to answer them, for even though he knew it looked like a contradiction to his behavior throughout the rest of the year, he felt that this changing of the lawn's color once a year was very important to him.

❧ The Trial

Pesach was over. Nat returned to his loneliness, to pain and longing. Before he could even recover slightly, a brown envelope arrived in his mailbox containing the court summons: "The State of Israel vs. Netanel Zimmerman," it read. "Charge: False accusations." The trial was set for a month later.

Nat looked at the summons for a long time, and during those moments felt a deep animosity for anyone calling himself *charedi* — especially if his name was Shimon Domb.

It was Nat Zimmerman's most embattled month. Of course, he made sure not to do anything which might lead to his arrest; aside from this, he did everything in his power to promote the excavations of the archaeologists and to provoke the members of Sacred Sites. He threw money around, spending it on provocative notices and posters. Nat didn't limit himself, though, to opposing only the members of Sacred Sites but expanded his circle to include the entire religious public. And if we would read what was written on those notices and posters, there is no doubt we would discover that Nat hated the Torah- and mitzvah-observant as much as he hated enemy nations, and perhaps even more so.

During one of those demonstrations against the members of Sacred Sites, someone called out to Nat: "What do you have against us? Are you sure you're not carrying this too far? Are you out of your mind?"

Nat didn't have to think too far to realize that the person shouting was none other than his opponent Shimon Domb.

The day of the trial arrived. Nat sat stiffly in the courtroom. His lawyer attempted a defense which, in the face of photographic and even filmed proof presented by the prosecution to the court, proved ineffective. The judge's expression was also not very encouraging, and during recess, Nat's lawyer whispered that he might be able to substitute public service for time in jail.

As soon as the words were spoken, Nat's face fell. He, Nat Zimmerman, fighter for freedom and progress would sit in jail like a common criminal. How would he be able to face life afterwards?

He sat brooding until the end of the break when the trial reached its final stages. But if Nat had thought that the worst was behind him, he was in for a surprise, for his lawyer informed him that none other than his archenemy, Shimon Domb, the one who had pressed charges against him, was about to take the stand.

Nat returned to the courtroom and flashed a hate-filled glance at the witness stand, behind which Shimon Domb already stood.

"The witness for the prosecution, Shimon Domb, please," declared the judge.

Shimon Domb took the stand and began to describe the activities of the Sacred Sites organization. He talked about respect for the living and respect for the dead, about the importance of honoring the dead and the sanctity of Jewish graves, and explained how archaeologists were so coarsely trampling on those sacred values.

At this point, the judge tried to stop him and remind him why he had come, but Shimon only nodded his head and said, "It has to do with that. I'll get to the main point in a minute."

He did get there but not at all to the matter about which he had asked to testify. Shimon began to cry out, "I accuse," against the government, against the police, against the archaeologists, and concluded with the fervent hope that all would come to their senses and understand the importance of preserving the graves of our ancestors.

As Shimon was about to step down from the stand, the irate judge said, "Wait a minute! What about your complaint against Nat Zimmerman?"

For a split second Shimon looked at him blankly, then, as if remembering, said, "Oh, him? The complaint isn't against him but against the police who don't try to ascertain the truth but only rush to arrest the *charedi* demonstrator even if he is the one being attacked."

The prosecutor, who felt victory slipping from his hands, interrupted and asked, "And what about Zimmerman's trumped-up charges against you?"

"I don't blame him," Shimon told the startled courtroom. "I think he's a reasonable person but even reasonable people forget themselves in the heat of an argument. Have you ever seen anyone fighting who thinks he's the one who started? This man has reasons of his own for his war, and they have no connection at all with the archaeological excavations. I hope he understands that he is mistaken and will decide that if he's already fighting it might as well be on the right side. But I wouldn't recommend condemning him for pressing false charges the way I would suggest bringing to trial the heads of the police . . . "

Nat thought he was dreaming. He looked again and again at his eternal enemy and couldn't believe the man. He was going to be the one who would save him from this seemingly hopeless situation?

The judge leaned forward. He looked furious. "Do you mean to tell us that you made us all come here solely to listen to your lecture?"

Shimon looked at the judge and couldn't understand the anger. "I want to call the police to the stand and accuse them of discrimination," he cried out.

"Leave the stand!" roared the judge as he banged down his gavel. "I hereby declare the accused not guilty of all charges! Will the claimant please step into my chambers . . . "

Nat remained rooted to his place, unable to comprehend what had prompted Shimon Domb to do what he did. He stretched his imagination to try to find some favor he had done for Shimon to justify his behavior but couldn't find any. He came to the simple conclusion that Shimon had gone out of his way to save him, and he couldn't figure out why. The thought gave him no rest.

He left the courtroom in a complete daze when suddenly he spotted Shimon Domb. "If you . . . if you think that I intend to stop battling you, you're wrong. You won't manage to buy me off with tricks. You won't succeed — why are you smiling?"

Shimon Domb just looked at him and smiled. "Did I ask you for anything?" he asked quietly, adding, "I was brought up to speak only the truth. Think it over. Isn't that exactly what I did? Especially the part about your motives for demonstrating against us."

For some reason, these remarks infuriated Nat even more, and he vented his wrath on Shimon and all those like him.

๛ Meaningful Enmity

The following week, Nat again appeared at a demonstration at a new excavation site, and once more, he found himself face to face with Shimon Domb.

This happened the next day as well, and soon enough, reporters, photographers, police and archaeologists all knew that there would be no archaeological excavation anyplace where there had once been a cemetery without the presence of these two and without their arguments in blasting tones. The police treated Shimon and Nat like permanent fixtures at every excavation, anywhere in the country, during the hours of day or night... or at any other hours.

Neither Nat nor Shimon noticed that their arguments since the trial had become more to the point and less personal. This became apparent to Nat only when Shimon failed to appear at one of the demonstrations along with the dozens of protesters who came each and every time, and Nat found himself instinctively searching for the young man with the black beard and listening for his voice. He didn't find him, though. This was the first time Nat felt bored at a demonstration.

At the next demonstration, when he asked Shimon, "Did you give up?" Shimon explained that he had taken his mother for some kind of medical treatment. As to Nat's question of why his father didn't take her, Shimon explained that he had taken his mother everywhere for the past thirteen years since his father had passed away. Nat found himself stammering an apology. Shimon reassured him that there was no need to apologize because although his words had made him sad, they hadn't been hurtful.

Then Shimon recalled why he had come and began to shout, "Robbers, remove your hands from these sacred bones," while Nat shouted back at him, "Make way for progress. Let the scientists develop the world," and all of the other slogans he knew so well.

That demonstration was one of the stormiest in their history, and when it ended, the demonstrators, along with

Rabbi Spiegel, climbed into their van for the return home —
all except for Shimon Domb.

"You missed your ride," taunted Nat.

"I didn't miss it. I'm staying here to make sure the
archaeologists don't violate the restrictions imposed on
them. I know them well, and I know that they're just waiting
for us to go before they start poking around the graves."

"In that case, I'll stay here, too, to demonstrate
against you," Nat told him. "I won't leave these scientific
excavations in your hands."

The two remained behind, watching each other.
Suddenly, black clouds covered the sky, and rain began to
pour down in torrents. At first the archaeologists tried to
continue working but when the downpour grew heavier,
they fled to their van for shelter.

Nat opened the umbrella he had brought with him,
while Shimon, who never carried an umbrella, took doubt-
ful shelter under a tree. Of course the tree did not offer
much protection against the pounding hail, and Shimon
soon discovered that not only rain was falling on him but a
shower of leaves as well.

"Take a look at yourself, you idiot," Nat cried out to
him. But Shimon was waiting for the archaeologists to
leave.

After about an hour, the archaeologists gave up and
drove away. The setting sun streaked the sky a blazing red.
The excavation site appeared abandoned and deep puddles
covered the earth. Shimon began to walk toward the road.

"Where are you going now?" Nat shouted.

"I have to get to Bnei Brak," Shimon replied.

"Where will you find a bus at this time in such a deserted place?"

"It'll be okay," Shimon said. "Anyway, do I have a
choice?"

He continued slogging through the mud on his way to the road, a small drum pounding in his head. He began to feel very nauseous. He placed his hand, shaking from the cold, on his forehead. It was burning.

Out of the blue he heard Nat's voice. "Wait a minute. I'm going anyway with the tractor — I'll take you to where you can get a ride."

Shimon turned around, a look of amazement on his face.

"Just because you're a fool doesn't mean you have to get sick as well," shouted Nat angrily as he climbed up on the tractor and turned on the motor.

Shimon got on the tractor, and the two rode off without exchanging a word. One glance at Shimon and Nat didn't need a doctor's degree to know that the man was ill.

"Do you think anyone will agree to take you on the bus?" Nat asked. "You look like a waterfall."

"What should I do?" asked Shimon.

"Listen," Nat struggled to put his thoughts into words, "I live ten minutes from here, and I have a lot of bedrooms. You can sleep in one of them until the morning."

If Shimon was taken aback by the suggestion, he managed to conceal his surprise quite well. He nodded his head and sunk into the seat, exhausted.

The tractor came to a stop. "This is my house," said Nat curtly. Shimon hastily got himself together and dragged himself into the house.

Once inside, Nat turned on the heater and gave Shimon a pair of pajamas so that he could hang up his wet clothing. Shimon felt a deep lethargy spread through his limbs. He didn't feel well at all, yet through the haze of pain, he knew that Nat was giving him some tea and an aspirin. He drew the cup close to his lips and then hesitated. "The cup is kosher, nudnik," he heard Nat's irritated voice from afar.

Shimon recited a blessing, sipped from the cup and washed down the pill. Then he recited Shema... and fell asleep.

When he awoke he felt better. He got out of bed and then remembered that his tefillin weren't with him because he had expected to go home. He worried about how he would be able to find a pair of tefillin in a place like this.

Nat, who had just entered the room, solved the problem. "I have a pair of tefillin which belonged to my father. He left them for me, to no purpose. Wait a minute and I'll bring them to you."

Nat returned to the room with his father's precious tefillin, and Shimon couldn't help but say, "See, it wasn't 'to no purpose.' "

Shimon dressed and prayed alone. He finished and prepared to go when he heard Nat ask him, "Where are you going now?"

Shimon hesitated slightly. "There's a demonstration at the excavations near the Ayalon River. I have to be there."

Nat, who had also planned on attending that demonstration, asked, "How do you intend to get there?"

"Don't worry," Shimon replied. "Providence takes care of things like that."

"Look," Nat said, "I'm going there too. I can take you."

At the excavation site near the Ayalon River, one of the policeman looked at his watch. "Interesting. It's pretty quiet here today. Rabbi Spiegel's group didn't come, and neither did that *moshavnik* — what's his name? Zimmerman. Even that troublemaker Domb didn't come, which means a quiet day, no?"

"There's the *moshavnik*," said another policeman, pointing to the old tractor crawling toward the excavations.

"Okay, the three of us will be bored here together," said the first.

The tractor drew closer and stopped. Nat climbed down slowly, and the policemen rubbed their eyes when they saw who climbed down after him.

Shimon raced toward the archaeologists, who had already begun to dig, shouting, "Stop desecrating the graves!"

Nat Zimmerman ran alongside him, crying, "An end to religious coercion!"

The two policemen, who had witnessed plenty in their lives, got a shock at the sight of one of the strangest things they had ever seen.

৯ Nat and Shimon

Shimon liked the new transportation arrangement and, as a result, agreed to sleep at Nat's house anytime there was a demonstration in the area. At those opportunities they found themselves talking about everything — and a bit more.

At a subsequent demonstration, Shimon delicately asked Nat why in forty-seven years he had never married. Nat replied with a sigh that the opportunity to do so simply hadn't come his way. He found himself telling Shimon about his *charedi* family, and the surprised Shimon replied that in his wildest dreams he had never imagined that Nat even knew anyone who kept Torah and mitzvos.

The conversation ended when the police began to chase dozens of black-hatted demonstrators who had neared the excavation site, and Shimon, seeing that the police had moved away from him, inched towards the diggings, clung to one of the boulders and shouted, "Robbers!" until the policemen returned and dragged him away too.

Pressured by the members of Sacred Sites, the Ministry of Religious Affairs ordered the excavation site closed. With that, Sacred Sites scored another victory, something Nat decided should never be allowed to happen.

They met again at a new excavation site in Beit She'an, and between one argument and the next, Nat asked Shimon why *he* had never married. Shimon shrugged his shoulders and found no words to answer him. Nat decided not to trouble him with further questions.

That evening, when the two were seated in Nat's living room, Shimon suddenly burst out with the answer to the question Nat had posed to him earlier that day. He told him about his childhood, about why he hadn't found himself in the yeshivah, about his joining Sacred Sites, and about the reluctance of young women to marry him because of his activities. Here and there Nat tried to help him out with suggestions but he soon realized that he couldn't be much help to him in the matter. As a result, he made do with a declaration. "If they would ask me, I would recommend you with all my heart. I would even let my own daughter marry a good-hearted boy like you. It's only too bad that I don't have any."

Shimon's eyes filled with tears, since he had never heard words like those from anyone except his mother.

❧ *The Shidduch*

Spring came and Pesach knocked on Nat's door. The small house prepared itself to host the growing family. And who do you think helped him, between demonstrations, if not Shimon Domb?

When the work was finished and the house was ready, Nat told Shimon how happy he was to see his large family still close to him, still coming to visit him. At these words, he saw a shadow pass across Shimon's face.

"I have no family," he said. "My mother and I sit at the Seder table alone, and it's one of the saddest times of the year for us."

Nat was sorry he had spoken and immediately invited Shimon and his mother to join them for the Seder. Shimon was adamant in his refusal, and all of Nat's attempts to persuade him to change his mind were in vain.

When Shimon returned home, Nat began to reflect on the joy he derived from those once-a-year visits of his family, when they descended on him for seven days and seven nights. Suddenly he realized that the day those visits would stop was the day any taste left in his life would disappear — for quite some time ago Nat had reached the conclusion that there wasn't much taste in his life, and what there was, was as bitter as death.

Pesach arrived in the blink of an eye. Nat had managed to ready the house in time, and when he saw his beloved family descending from the chartered bus which had brought them all, his joy knew no bounds. Only one thing saddened him — as it did his oldest brother, Shmuel.

It had to do with Shoshana, Shmuel's oldest daughter. She was exceptionally talented but nonetheless, or perhaps precisely because of it, she had remained unmarried. And if at first the matter had been greeted with a smile by the family, when she reached the age of twenty-five, the smiles faded and turned to real worry, which intensified over time. This year when Shoshana arrived Nat was both happy to see her and yet sad to see that she was still able to come, for the married children no longer came to Nat's home for Pesach.

Suddenly, a brilliant idea flashed across his mind. Taking his brother Shmuel aside, he told him excitedly, "I have a wonderful boy for your daughter, Shoshana."

Shmuel looked at him and gently explained that Shoshana preferred a Torah- and mitzvah-observant boy who studied in a yeshivah all day, or at least set aside times for daily Torah study. Nat cut him short with a laugh. "Don't worry, I had no intention of suggesting one of the *moshavnikim*. The boy I have in mind comes from an excellent home and is one hundred percent *charedi*."

Shmuel looked at him as if to say, "How does Nat come to know a boy like that?"

Nat began to tell him about Shimon Domb, extolling his virtues, and, like a veteran *shadchan*, suggested that Shmuel ask Rabbi Spiegel and an impressive number of other rabbis whose names he had picked up from his arguments with Shimon. "Even Rabbi Wasserman knows him," he added.

Shmuel's eyebrows went up. Rabbi Wasserman was one of the *gedolei hador*, and the fact that he knew Shimon sounded quite impressive.

Afraid that others might get there first, Shmuel called here and even there and in the end declared, "There is what to talk about."

This announcement prompted Nat to call Shimon's mother and inform her that she should come as quickly as possible to the moshav and stay for Pesach. If at first she refused to hear of it, she was soon persuaded by Nat's argument that this might be her last chance to see any *nachas* from her only son. Convinced by this, she told him, "We're on our way." And if at first Shimon protested vigorously, after his mother announced that she was going, he had no choice but to join her.

It was only on the second day of Pesach that Shimon and Shoshana had a chance to talk, and if at first Shoshana was positive that there was no chance that a boy considered "an activist" would suit her, she soon found out that in this case, and in this case only, the rule did not apply. Shoshana, like Shimon, didn't need any other cases. The decision by majority vote was: marriage.

They broke this news first to the *shadchan*, and then to their parents. The roof of the old house almost flew away from the happiness and excitement bubbling within.

At the end of the Pesach holiday, the family, including the bride-to-be and her parents, returned home. Shimon and his mother arrived from their nearby lodgings in order to thank their host for his wonderful hospitality, not to mention the extraordinary kindness he had done for them.

Nat stood at the window and followed them with his gaze, but before the familiar sorrow of parting had begun to overcome him, he saw Shimon whisper something to his mother and then rush back towards the house.

Nat led him to the living room, where Shimon spoke to him alone.

"Listen, Zimmerman, I still haven't thanked you enough — perhaps because I'm bothered by an idea which gives me no rest. It will sound foolish to you, and you might even kick me out, but I have to tell you."

Nat waited expectantly and motioned Shimon to continue.

"Listen, Nat. I know what it means to live alone. After all, I've lived that way for thirty-one years. Now, thanks to you I have a *kallah*, and for that you have my appreciation and indebtedness for the rest of my life. But Nat, there's one more thing I'm missing..." Shimon found it hard to continue.

"I don't have a father."

Nat was astonished. He still didn't understand what Shimon was getting at.

"Zimmerman, you're alone, and my mother is alone as well. I thought... perhaps..."

Nat did not reply. His face flushed. No one had ever made an offer like this to him. But he was quickly brought back down to earth by Shimon's next words.

"My mother won't marry someone who isn't observant, so I thought to suggest that you. . . think about it."

"You're giving me a condition I can't fulfill," Nat cut him short.

"Really? Tell me, how many sins do you actually commit? Is it really so hard for you to keep the mitzvos?"

"Let's say that I would keep them. But if it's only because of pressure, what's the point?" asked Nat.

" 'From ulterior motives come pure motives,' " Shimon quoted. "True, my mother won't be overjoyed by such an idea, but I think it's a solution. After all, she can't remain alone. She's young at heart, as you surely noticed."

"Let me think about it," Nat told him. "I'll give you my answer later. Don't say a thing to your mother, because I doubt whether my reply will be in the affirmative. Not because of her, but because of the condition."

Shimon said good-bye and continued on his way.

A half a half-hour was all Nat needed to decide he wouldn't accept the offer. *A man of forty-eight can't change his ways, his opinions, and his habits. How would it look if I changed like that? Even worse, how could I face myself, knowing that I changed my opinions only because I feel so lonely?* he thought to himself.

Nat thought more about it and decided that he couldn't be different than what he was used to. He also didn't feel he had the emotional strength to make a change in his life. He decided to reject the offer, despite his fear of loneliness, and continue to make due with the yearly visits of his family in the future. After all, they didn't make any conditions. What was wrong with partial happiness?

At the next demonstration Nat informed Shimon that he couldn't accept his offer. He did it as politely as he could and said that if the condition were removed, there might be something to talk about.

Shimon's face reflected pain but also determination. Pain that for now, his mother would have to remain alone, yet determination in knowing that she would never agree to marry a man who was not observant.

They didn't bring up the subject again.

✎ *The Battle Over the House*

One morning, about a month after Pesach, Nat was awakened by a loud noise. Stepping outside, he saw huge bulldozers and numerous trucks all over the area. Nat was suspicious and went out to ask the drivers what they were doing.

"Haven't you heard about the trans-valley road?" one of the drivers shouted. "We're building you a great road, six lanes, the most modern road in the country."

"Uh, where will this road pass through?" Nat stammered.

The driver moved Nat aside and sketched an imaginary line through two hills straight through Nat's house.

"Impossible," cried Nat. "There's a house here, isn't there?"

"Take a good look at my bulldozer. In two minutes flat, it'll make mashed potatoes out of that house."

Nat bit his lips nervously. "But that house is mine!"

The driver looked at him in surprise. "Sorry, I didn't know. But don't worry, they'll compensate you. They'll give you a different home, worth more, in a new development."

"But I want *this* house."

The driver shrugged his shoulders. "That's life. I've met a lot of people like you. But what can you do? You can't stop progress."

Nat rushed home, sat down in his living room, and looked around. He sat like that for a long time. He knew what it meant: an end to the family visits — visits which were the focal point of his life, his reason for living.

He let out a choked scream and decided to fight.

First, he phoned the chairman of the county council, who lived on the moshav, and made an appointment to see him. It soon became clear that this fellow was one of the main promoters of the road. Nat pleaded with him to move the road over just a tiny bit, and even showed him how it could be done, but the chairman explained that Nat's plan would cost too much. Soon he switched from polite explanation to direct attack. "It's not like you, the champion of progress, to impede the development of the entire valley. What's the big deal? You'll get a nice house instead of that old dilapidated one. Why are you being so stubborn?"

Nat could explain what a great tragedy it would be for him and how it wasn't so much the destruction of the house as much as it was his inability to have his wonderful family stay with him — the only people close to him. He tried pleading and persuading, until at last, the chairman's patience snapped. "As far as I'm concerned, you can fight all you want," he said with exasperation, "but the matter is closed. Within a few weeks, you'll have to vacate your home."

Nat was shocked. Something in the chairman's voice made it clear that he had inside information that Nat didn't have. Nat decided to visit the council's department of planning and soon learned that his father, may he rest in peace, had long ago signed a waiver permitting the razing of the house in the event that a road would one day would be built through the property.

In other words, there was no hope.

Nat returned home in a state of depression. He sat down on his bed and burst into bitter tears. He looked around him and felt like screaming. He wept over his ruined, and now meaningless, life.

He tried to make a few phone calls, to use his connections, to talk with some archaeologists, hoping that they could pull strings for him. Some of them didn't even bother to answer him. Others listened politely, until he came to the part about the signed waiver, and then immediately interjected, "You don't have a chance. Don't waste your time. Anyway, what difference would it make to you to move to a smaller place — you don't even have a large family..."

Nat wanted to shout, "Yes, I do!" But he realized that they wouldn't understand, because they didn't care and had never cared!

The days passed, and Nat mourned. He didn't leave his house, he didn't shave, and he barely ate. He was undergoing a crisis, and had no one with whom he could share his feelings.

Every now and then, he would stalk the house like a caged lion, peering through the window at the bulldozers which were devouring the nearby hills and drawing closer to his house menacingly, only a mile and a half away.

On one of those "rounds," he found himself in the small room he had let Shimon Domb stay in on his visits. On the table lay the tefillin he had received from his father.

Haplessly, Nat found himself opening the bag and putting on the tefillin. He did this mechanically, without a drop of emotion, feeling like a drowning man, grasping.... By the time he realized what he was doing, he had the tefillin on, and the straps encircling his head and pressing into his arm gave him a sense of security.

He removed the tefillin quickly and placed them in their bag. Then he began to think about the option he had so easily dismissed: Shimon Domb's suggestion.

On the one hand, he lacked the emotional strength to do it; on the other hand, he had even less emotional strength to live his life all alone. He couldn't picture himself observing mitzvos mechanically, like the way he had just put on the tefillin. How would it look? How would he see himself? But then, the loneliness and suffering... What would become of him?

If in the past Nat had measured this world against the next, and had preferred the former over the latter, he now saw that if he were to continue as he had been, he would lose this world as well as the next world — which he had worked so diligently at losing his whole life.

And that's what convinced him.

Now Nat had only one problem. How to do it. What about his self-respect? How could he just do an about-face on his entire life? He felt he didn't have the strength for it.

Engrossed in his thoughts, he found himself outside, walking down the path from his house to the road. Suddenly he decided, *If I get a sign from Above, I'll give up my entire lifestyle and turn over a new leaf, and even marry Shimon's mother; but without such a sign, I can't. I simply won't be able to.*

As he walked, he turned his gaze to the heavens and didn't notice the bulldozer coming towards him, getting dangerously close.

A screech of brakes was heard. The bulldozer halted right near his nose, and Nat fell back in fright.

Before he had even managed to stand up, he heard the driver shout, "Are you crazy? Do you think you have to join the dead in order to protect them?"

Nat blinked, not understanding what the driver meant. "What dead?"

Then he saw a group of black-hatted men carrying placards, standing not far from him.

Out of the group came Shimon Domb, running toward Nat. Helping him up, he shouted, "Zimmerman, they found an old cemetery beside your house. Don't think that this will stop us from protesting against the paving of the road. True, you are my *shadchan*, and I am very grateful to you, but don't expect that because of that I'll forgo defending the sanctity of the dead. You can protest against us as much as you want, but the trans-valley road won't pass through here, no matter what! Progress or no progress. We have a comprehensive plan to divert the road by a few miles. I'm telling you, Nat, this time our friendship won't help. What do you say?"

❧ Epilogue

It was a very modest ceremony. In the presence of a minyan of ten men, Netanel Zimmerman pronounced for the first time in his life those special words said under the wedding canopy. The guests found it difficult to hold back their tears.

The ceremony took place in the beautiful back yard of the old house. A table laden with drinks and baked delicacies had been placed in the large garden. Nat walked around in a daze, filled with joy and happiness, warmly responding to the blessings showered upon him.

Shimon and Shoshana, whose wedding had taken place only three weeks before, were still as happy as a new bride and groom.

Nat walked off by himself and strode toward the end of the large plot of land. He gazed out at the trans-valley road, which extended toward his house and then suddenly turned aside and continued on past the hills. Shafts of light streamed from the windows of his home and fell near the turn in the road. Suddenly, Nat knew that the story of the house was the story of his life, and that the turn in the road symbolized the turnabout in his life.

Nat began to cry without understanding the meaning of his tears. His weeping intensified but no one heard him, except for the hills and the turning road.

Something in his life was about to change.

A boulder fell and crumbled to bits on the newly paved road, and in Nat's heart as well.

He turned around and walked slowly back to the house, to the old house on the moshav.

Pay Heed
to the
Soul

S ounds of destruction — the rumbling of bulldozers, the droning of tractors and the
pounding of sledgehammers tearing down the
buildings slated for demolition — reached the ears of Tuvia
Grossness, president of Manhattan's Beth Aharon Synagogue.

Seated in his narrow cubbyhole, the shul's "office,"
he reread once again the letter he had received that very
morning: "Mr. Tuvia Grossness, Beth Aharon Synagogue,
regarding the evacuation of the synagogue prior to its
demolition.

"On behalf of our client, Maiden Star, I hereby inform you that you must vacate your synagogue by the first
of June of this year. On that date, demolition will com-
mence." It was signed by Henry Appendyke, the attorney
for Maiden Star, Inc.

In truth, Reb Tuvia hadn't been surprised by the letter. The synagogue, and thousands of other antiquated structures in the area, had for a long time belonged to the corporation, which had bought the land on which they stood with the intention of tearing them down and erecting in their stead skyscrapers to house tens of thousands of offices, hotels and businesses.

The synagogue was in the heart of the section slated for reconstruction, and there was no doubt that it would be razed. When its original owner, Reb Simchah Meyer Zilberstein, had purchased it, he had stipulated that the synagogue's present location was to be temporary and that it would eventually need to be relocated. Reb Simchah Meyer was an astute businessman and had foreseen the financial potential of that section of the city. Displaying rare business acumen, he had predicted that within a number of decades the value of his property would increase a hundred times over. Reality had far exceeded his expectations.

Along with the condition he had made, Reb Simchah Meir included in his will instructions to his descendants to set aside part of the profits they would make from future construction on the property to be used for relocation of the synagogue.

But had Reb Simchah Meyer ever dreamed that his very own children and grandchildren would stray from traditional Judaism? Had he ever dreamed that they would treat the will with scorn, hiring a lawyer to claim in court that "an antiquated religious document" did not obligate them?

Despite the repeated attempts of the synagogue's attorney to force the grandchildren to honor Reb Simcha's will, the court ruled that the will had no legal validity because it had been signed only by the rabbi of the synagogue, Rabbi Moskowitz, and its president, Moshe Grossness, both of whom had died and whose signatures could thus not be verified.

The legal battle had failed. The letter which lay on Reb Tuvia's desk was proof of that.

This is the end, reflected Reb Tuvia, a lump in his throat. He felt like crying. The tremendous clamor he had been hearing recently bore witness to the fact that the process of demolition had indeed begun, and this letter now announced that within a few months the tractors would reach the synagogue where he, his father, and his grand-father had served as president, and for whose sake they had sacrificed their time, money, and energy.

In two months, all would become an isle of desolation. And funds for an alternate building were nonexistent.

He recalled the file which contained his grand-father's will. "The day will yet come when you will have to spend a great deal of time deciphering the contents of this file," Tuvia's father had told him on his deathbed.

Now is the time, thought Reb Tuvia as he began to search for the file among the piles of accounts, receipts, and lists of income and expenditures which crowded his tiny office.

After a half-hour's search, the file, apparently untouched for forty years, was found. Coughing from the thick dust which covered it, Reb Tuvia hastened to open its covers. Old, yellowed pages appeared before his eyes. He immediately recognized the original copy of the will which hadn't been of much help. Attached to the file was a blueprint of the synagogue and a map of the area with various plots of land outlined. Reb Tuvia's gaze fell on one plot in particular, in the heart of the district, which had been circled. In the center was a large question mark.

The last page of the file contained only ten lines and was written in Hebrew. Mentally translating it into English, Reb Tuvia read it aloud:

In order not to uproot the planted,
Do not take my request for granted;
A man named Yehoshua you must seek
And spend with him an entire week.

In a city which hills surround,
The desired treasure will be found.

In the place where Yitzchak reaped his seed,
The feelings of your heart you'll heed.
At the home of Yitzchak Short you'll rest,
And with the "flower" discover your behest.

❑ ❑ ❑

In the luxurious offices of Maiden Star, Inc., the president, Josh S., sat brooding.

His expression was grim. A huge project he had initiated was about to collapse, and all because of a relatively small fifteen-acre piece of land, whose owner, an unknown company called C. M., registered in Panama, had refused to cooperate in the project. Josh's lawyers had told him quite candidly that C. M.'s legal procedures were likely to hold up the project for a number of years, something which would affect the liquidity of the company and might even cause it to go bankrupt. Josh instructed them to locate the owners of the company immediately and to purchase the plot from them at all costs. He quickly learned, though, that the owners of the company insisted on maintaining anonymity, and that their lawyers, among the most famous and highly respected in New York, had politely, yet firmly, notified Josh's representatives that under no circumstances would they agree to sell the property.

Leaning on his desk, Josh tried to devise a plan. After a few long moments, he rose and headed towards the company's archives with the vague hope of finding documents which might lead him to the owners of the mysterious C. M. company.

He sat there an entire day. He went through the records of hundreds of deals with various landowners, recalling with a smile the hopeless struggle of the Orthodox Jews who, waving a useless religious document, had hoped that the inheritors of a certain plot of land would provide them with the funds to replace their synagogue. Josh recalled the ease with which his top-notch attorney had vanquished the small-time lawyers of the Orthodox plaintiffs. The image of an old Orthodox Jew named Tuvia, who had burst into the Maiden Star offices one day and had managed to murmur a few sentences in Yiddish before he was thrown out by security guards, flashed through his mind. *Those were the days*, mused Josh before he turned to the next document.

He did not find any reference to C. M.

The hours passed, twilight fell, and the pale rays of the sun flickered in Josh's eyes when he chanced upon an old file. He opened it, his eyes immediately drawn to the question mark on the first page, right in the heart of the problematic plot of land owned by C. M. Josh felt the pounding of his heart and the moistness of the palms of his hands.

Quickly, he proceeded to the second document in the file, and there his eyes were caught by a page on which ten lines were written in a language whose letters were familiar to him but not so familiar that he could understand what was written.

Josh lifted the telephone and shouted into the receiver: "Get me Dave Kahan." Within an hour, he and his childhood friend were sitting together. Although Josh and

David had studied in different schools, they had met every Sunday in Sunday school.

When the two graduated elementary school, their ways parted. David began to study in an Orthodox institution called a yeshivah, while he, Josh, was sent to university. Their friendship, although fairly tenuous, remained.

Josh, who recognized the Hebrew writing of the document, immediately thought of David, who was an expert in riddles and word puzzles. That's why he had asked his secretary to call David urgently.

David translated what was written:

So that you will not be poor and low,
With the "big miracle" to Zion please go.
On the top floor of the French courtyard you'll dwell
And there hear the sounds your heart knows so well.

The voice of reason to you will speak
When the solution of this riddle you will seek.

One night the loneliness will break,
And the strains of a melody cause you to quake.
Hearken to your soul
For beside the "*shoshan*" lies your goal.

David looked at the document for a long time, only to realize that he didn't understand a word of it. "I'll break my head over it at home," he said. Then, taking a photocopy of the riddle, he left.

❑ ❑ ❑

Reb Tuvia Grossness sat quietly in the synagogue. "In order not to uproot the planted," the riddle said. But who is Yehoshua? What is, "In a city which hills surround"? Switzerland? Perhaps.

Reb Tuvia searched his mind but could find no answer. He despaired but only for a moment. He tried to think logically. Maybe he should first of all try to find out who this Yehoshua was. Because the author of the riddle was Reb Simchah Meir Zilberstein, the synagogue's founder, Reb Tuvia assumed that it must be one of his descendants. It would be easy enough to find out. Reb Tuvia leafed through the synagogue's ledgers. Reb Simchah Meir had several sons. His eldest, Menachem, had died at a young age. The second son was named Michael.

The ledger noted a bris which had been held thirty-five years ago for an infant named Yehoshua. However, Reb Tuvia found no further references to that same Yehoshua, neither occasions celebrated nor donations made. Reb Tuvia realized that the Jewish name of this Yehoshua must have been solely ceremonial.

In vain, Reb Tuvia searched the telephone book under the name "Zilberstein," failing to find either a Jewish or a Christian name resembling "Yehoshua." His eyes nearly closed, when suddenly an idea occurred to him. Perhaps this Yehoshua hadn't liked his last name, either? Rapidly, Reb Tuvia flipped through the pages until he reached the letter *S* and the name "Silberstein." There it was. Not Yehoshua but a similar name: "Silberstein, Josh; Maiden Star."

Suddenly, everything fell into place.

Reb Tuvia's hands began to tremble. Beads of moisture formed on his forehead and rolled down his cheeks — or were they tears? He forgot the lateness of the hour and dialed the number.

A drowsy voice answered. "Hello?"

"Is this Josh Silberstein?" asked Reb Tuvia, not noticing the anger in the voice which answered.

"Yes."

"This is Tuvia, the president of the synagogue. Do you remember me? I wanted to... Hello... Hello..."

Click.

❏ ❏ ❏

The next morning, Josh again sat with David. "I think I've solved a small but important part of the riddle," David told him. "You must set out for Israel with a person called '*Nes HaGadol*' and there find a place called 'the French court.'"

"Who is this '*Nes HaGadol*'?" asked Josh.

" '*Nes*' means 'miracle' in Hebrew. '*Gadol*' means 'big.' Did you ever come across anyone with a last name like that?"

" 'Big Miracle'?" Josh repeated. "No."

The telephone rang. Josh lifted the receiver, listened for a moment, and slammed it down angrily.

"It's that nuisance Tuvia Grossness again. I thought I had already gotten rid of him."

"Tuvia what?" David asked.

"Grossness. An old man who, shall we say, pesters me. He called —"

"Fool," David cut him short. " '*Gross*' means 'big' in Yiddish. 'Big miracle' is Grossness, the man the riddle is talking about!"

Reb Tuvia sat in his office in total despair. Twice the receiver had been slammed down on him.

But then, why should anyone agree to listen to him? Even the will had been ignored by the beneficiaries.

The telephone rang but Reb Tuvia made no rush to answer it. When he finally lifted the receiver, he heard, "This is Josh Silberstein, and I think we should meet."

They met that very day. After each had explained how he had found the other, Josh declared, "I don't like you, and you don't like me. Nonetheless, I presume we have no choice but to search together for the mysterious C. M. company in Israel. You need me for your synagogue, and I need you for my project."

Tuvia nodded.

"But I have no idea to which city the riddle refers," added Josh.

"I've already solved that problem," said Reb Tuvia. "The riddle I have says, 'In a city which hills surround...' It's written in *Tehillim*, 'Yerushalayim, mountains surround her.'"

Josh lifted the receiver. "Book me two places on the next flight to Israel." The two packed their bags hastily and departed that very night.

Throughout the flight, Tuvia pored over a small *Chumash*. Josh tapped him on the shoulder. "Do you have any idea to which neighborhood the riddle is referring?" he asked. "Mine says we must live in a certain neighborhood in Yerushalayim but aren't there quite a few?"

"Mine says which neighborhood," Reb Tuvia replied.

"And you won't tell me?" asked Josh suspiciously.

"It says, '...where Yitzchak reaped his seed.' I think it's talking about Yitzchak in *Bereshis*, chapter 26, verse 12, where it's written: 'Yitzchak planted seed in that land, and he found... a hundredfold,'" Tuvia translated.

Josh didn't understand.

"Don't you get it? 'A hundredfold' is Meah She'arim," Reb Tuvia said excitedly.

"But where?" Josh asked, being careful not to say a word about the "French courtyard."

"When we get to Meah She'arim we'll see," decided Reb Tuvia.

When the two landed in Israel it was late afternoon. "Let's hurry," said Josh.

But Tuvia told him, "I have to *daven minchah* and *ma'ariv*."

"I'll wait."

"I need a *minyan*," Tuvia noted. "If you don't help me out, it will take a long time."

And so, Josh Silberstein, owner of a large New York company, found himself asking the passengers rushing to collect their baggage to join the *minchah* service. "Excuse me, sir," he tapped one of them on the shoulder. "*Minchah*."

To Josh's surprise, the man who turned around was none other than Barney Smith, a famous New York reporter.

"*Minchah* you said?" Barney repeated with raised eyebrows, recognizing the president of Maiden Star.

"No," Josh stammered. "Listen, this man asked me..." Josh turned around but Tuvia was gone. "Where did he disappear to?"

Barney shot him a look of bemused astonishment. Josh watched with embarrassment as Barney, skeptical, turned and left.

A moment later, Josh spotted Reb Tuvia, surrounded by nine other men.

"Where did you disappear to?" Josh asked him angrily, but Reb Tuvia could not pause from his prayers to answer.

Prayers over, the two left the airport and entered a taxi headed for Yerushalayim.

Josh brooded the entire way. He suspected that Reb Tuvia was trying to hide something from him in order to solve the riddle first. *No,* he thought. *I won't let him get away with it. From now on, I'll watch his every move.*

The taxi wended its way through the narrow streets of Meah She'arim. "Where should I stop?" the driver asked.

Silence.

"Where do you have to go?" he repeated with irritation.

"I don't know," said Reb Tuvia. "I simply don't know."

"We need the 'French courtyard' — *Chatzer HaTzorfatim*," recited Josh haltingly from the copy of the riddle he was holding.

"You probably mean *Chatzer Pariz* — Paris courtyard," said the driver, as he turned into a narrow alleyway. "It's at the end of the Batei Hungarin neighborhood."

In less than a minute, the taxi stopped next to an empty lot surrounded by a fence. "This is *Chatzer Pariz*," said the driver as he took his fee and drove off.

"My grandfather wanted us to live in this trap for a week?" Josh asked wearily.

"Not necessarily," replied Tuvia. "I assume he wanted us to stay somewhere in this neighborhood. At the home of someone the riddle I have refers to as '*katzar*.' This could either be 'Short' or 'Kurtz.' "

A young boy riding a stick passed by. The stick didn't have any wheels but that didn't stop the child from pretending it was a bus. The noise he made was comparable.

"Excuse me," Reb Tuvia asked him. "Do you know the Short family?"

The child replied in the negative.

"What about the Kurtz family?" Reb Tuvia attempted.

The child furrowed his brow. "You must mean Kurtzweil. They live upstairs, two houses away from the steps."

"On the top floor," quoted Josh from the riddle.

The two hurried up the old staircase with its carved banister. They soon found themselves opposite an arched door on which the name "Kurtzweil" appeared. They knocked hesitantly. A tall, heavyset man with black, penetrating eyes opened it.

"Excuse me," Reb Tuvia began in Yiddish. "My name is Tuvia Grossness, and my friend's name is Josh Silberstein. We were told to spend a week in this house. Please try to understand — we have a copy of a riddle which says, 'On the top floor of the French courtyard... at the home of the Yitzchak Short.' 'Short' means..." Suddenly he paused, realizing how ridiculous he sounded.

A strange expression crossed the man's face. Without saying a word, he turned around and disappeared into the house.

Five long minutes of bewilderment passed for the pair. In the end, the man reappeared in the doorway. His beard and clothing were white from the dust which clung to them. In his hand, he held an old note which had grown yellow with age. He looked at it.

"So," he said, raising his eyes to look at them. "Come in."

Reb Tuvia took the note. Two names were written on it in English: "Grossness," and "Zilberstein."

"Who gave you this note?" Josh asked after the first shock had subsided.

"It was sent to my father about forty years ago by an American friend of Hungarian origin who had supported Batei Hungarin Kollel for many years. This apartment actually belongs to the *kollel*, and it is not only my duty but also my pleasure to honor your small request."

"Who was that friend?" Josh asked.

"His name was Reb Simchah Meir Zilberstein. A relative of yours, I presume."

"My grandfather," replied Josh, noticing the look of shock in the eyes of his host at Josh's non-religious appearance.

Twilight fell. The two joined the Kurtzweils for supper. Josh was amazed to hear that all the numerous children sitting around the table actually belonged to one family. However, he made no comment on the subject. The meal ended, and the two went to their room to sleep.

Before falling asleep, Josh managed to see that Reb Tuvia had changed his regular yarmulke for a large white one and was swaying back and forth beside the window, chanting a pleasant and strange melody. Josh dozed off.

When he awoke in the morning, he sensed he was alone in the room. He dressed quickly and rushed to the kitchen, where some members of the household were already seated. "Where is Tuvia?" he asked in a panic.

"Yankele, take the guest to shul," Mrs. Kurtzweil commanded one of her children. The child took the guest and began to march down the winding alleys so familiar to him and so strange to the guest.

They reached the shul, where Josh met Reb Tuvia, who was wrapped in tallis and tefillin. Without his asking, a large yarmulke was placed on Josh's head. Someone wrapped a tallis around him, and a third person began to put tefillin on him. They did this as if it was understood, and Josh made no attempt to resist.

A few days passed. Josh began to show signs of impatience. He had no idea how, in the middle of the night, he would suddenly hear the "melody" to which his grandfather had referred. Tuvia was also perplexed, and both of them sat for hours trying to solve this crucial part of the riddle. On the other hand, Josh discovered that the waiting period in the Kurtzweil home was very pleasant. Josh, who was accustomed to living in luxury, was amazed to discover people living in shocking simplicity, freed from the competition and struggle for social status so characteristic of the society in which he lived. Nevertheless, he still regarded the Kurtzweil family coldly, as if he were an anthropologist making a scientific study. The scenes he witnessed made no impression on his heart.

The days passed quickly. Shabbos arrived. After prayers, the two joined the Kurtzweil family for the meal. Josh was deeply impressed by scenes the likes of which he had never before experienced. Even though he felt this world as far removed from his own as east is from west, something within him stirred. In truth, the scenes Josh was witnessing did not please him. Quite the opposite. He was overcome by a sorrow whose meaning eluded him. On the rare occasions he had reflected on the subject called "religion," he had come to the conclusion that it was an archaic and depressing subject. Now these thoughts found confirmation in the form of the innocent children who recited the Torah lessons they had learned in their various schools. *What does he know about the world,* mused Josh, as he looked into the large eyes of the oldest child who was speaking. In his heart, Josh felt pity.

Suddenly, he realized that it wasn't the child he pitied but himself. And that it wasn't because of the children's innocence that he was sad but because of the loss of his own innocence. At that moment, neither scorn nor ridicule filled his heart but jealousy. Yet of what was he jealous? Of the Kurtzweils' poverty? Of their lack of worldliness? What was there to envy in this family? Had they accomplished anything in life? Were any of them as highly respected or esteemed as he was in America?

In a split second, though, the thought that his status in America meant nothing to this family flashed through his mind. Suddenly, he recalled that he — Josh the big businessman — was in this old-fashioned neighborhood because of a riddle he had to solve; otherwise, he would lose all his money! He, Josh the invincible, would lose his whole world.

He looked at the children who were singing without a trace of worry on their faces and, in an instant, understood. Although he could not put his feelings into words, he knew that during those moments he had learned something about the world, something about his own life.

He rose and retreated to his room without saying a word. There he found himself crying for no apparent reason — something he hadn't done in years.

And so he fell asleep.

He awoke before dawn. A distant, sad melody drifted into his room from the street. He sat up in bed, as if in a dream but soon realized that he wasn't dreaming. The melody was real.

"Hearken to the soul," a voice was heard singing from afar. Josh rushed to put on a robe and went out onto the balcony which overlooked the narrow alleyways of Batei Hungarin.

Someone was walking through the streets, that was certain. The voice drew near. The anonymous singer was singing a song Josh recognized, though he didn't know from where. All of a sudden, Josh noticed his lips murmuring words he did not understand:

I will thank the L-rd, Who searches hearts
When morning stars together sing.

And the refrain:

Pay heed to the soul...
Opal, agate and absinthe...

Suddenly he recalled the image of a bearded man who had sat beside his bed many years ago and sung to him that very same song.

The Yerushalmi singer drew closer. His voice was filled with longing and yearning. A wave of nostalgia overcame Josh, though he did not understand why.

Soon the singer became visible. He was heavyset, with a white beard. His voice rang out loud and clear:

A man worries about the loss of his wealth
But not about the loss of his years.
His wealth is of no avail;
His days never return.

Josh repeated the words as if in a trance. Who was that old man singing in the street? Who was the old man who had sat on his bed so many years ago and sung that same song, with the same melody? Then he remembered.

Zeidy! Zeidy Simchah!

A long-buried childhood memory surfaced and flooded his soul. Yes, his grandfather, Zeidy Simchah, whom he had so loved, the only person who had ever showered him with warmth and love. One day, he had vanished from his life. "He went where all the old people go," Josh's father had said dryly at the time.

Why did you leave me, my beloved zeidy...my beloved Zeidy Simchah, Josh's injured heart silently screamed. *Why?*

The street singer drew nearer and reached the balcony. His voice was pleasant and strong. Josh stared transfixed.

Suddenly, Josh felt he was not alone. His host, Reb Yitzchak Kurtzweil, was standing beside him. "That's Reb Yeedle Cohen," he said. "Every Shabbos morning before dawn he passes through the streets awakening people to rise for prayers. He sang even at the time of the Mandate, despite the curfew the British imposed. Despite their beatings, he continued to sing the very song he is singing today. Do you know what they call him? Reb Yeedle *Vaker*, 'Reb Yeedle the awakener.' "

Josh did not reply. He remained rooted to the spot, his gaze fixed on the back of the man who was slowly walking away.

"Jews, rise to serve the Creator," sang the man in his special voice.

I will thank the L-rd Who searches hearts
When morning stars together sing.

Followed by the refrain:

Pay heed to the soul...

That Shabbos, a deep and strange silence enveloped Josh. His eagerness to solve the riddle seemed to have been washed away by the wave after wave of vague longings and introspection which engulfed him.

When Shabbos ended, he and Reb Tuvia once again sat down again to try to decipher the riddle. Reb Tuvia mentioned the words of Reb Yeedle's melody. "I will thank the L-rd, Who searches hearts when morning stars together sing... Pay heed to the soul... "

"That's it!" cried Josh after the words had been translated into English. "Those are the words that appear in my copy of the riddle."

"Show me," cried Tuvia, and for the first time Josh wasn't afraid to do so. He no longer feared that Reb Tuvia might solve the riddle first and cheat him.

" 'Pay heed to the soul...opal, agate, and absinthe...' Do you know what it means?" asked Reb Tuvia and, expecting no answer, replied himself, " 'The desired treasure, precious stones' — is the riddle referring to a diamond treasure?"

"Perhaps," said Josh. "But my riddle says, 'For beside the 'shoshan' lies your goal' — something else we must decipher."

"Interesting," replied Reb Tuvia. "My riddle has the word 'flower': 'And with the "flower" discover your behest.' Did the writer mean flowers in general, or the *shoshanah*, 'rose'?"

For a long time, the two sat wrapped in their thoughts. Suddenly, Reb Tuvia rose, went over to the telephone, and dialed a number.

"Hello, Zecharya. This is Tuvia Grossness. Yes, I'm in *Eretz Yisrael*. Everything is fine. Listen, perhaps you know a diamond dealer named Rosenblum?"

The man on the other end, a well-known Jerusalem jeweler and diamond dealer, did not hesitate. "Rosenblum? He occupies an entire floor in the Ramat Gan diamond center."

Reb Tuvia completed the conversation and sat down.

"And so," he said at last, "we have solved the riddle. Now we must visit Rosenblum in the diamond center."

The very next morning, they contacted Rosenblum and arranged to meet him in his office.

The trip to Ramat Gan seemed long. They arrived at the diamond center, rode up to the tenth floor, stood in front of the door, and knocked.

The door opened to reveal a long table at which a group of men were seated. Two chairs were left unoccupied. The two were escorted to them and seated. The man at the head of the table then announced, "I hereby call to order the meeting of the board of directors of... the C. M. company."

Josh was shocked. He stared at the men sitting around the table, all of whom appeared Orthodox, and felt completely overwhelmed.

"I must open this meeting with a brief explanation to our two esteemed guests," the chairman began. "This company was established forty years ago by a very special man named Reb Simchah Meir Zilberstein. He began it for one main purpose, as well as for a number of secondary reasons. The main purpose: to insure the perpetuation of the Beth Aharon Synagogue, built in memory of, and named after, his father.

"Reb Meir Simcha's instructions explicitly stated that as long as the synagogue was not in jeopardy C. M. should not interfere on its behalf. In the meantime, the funds of the trust which Reb Simchah Meir established were to be used for charitable purposes and to support Torah. I must mention that the fund initially contained ten million dollars. Due to the wise investments made over the years by the people seated here it now totals hundreds of millions of dollars.

"The Trust also owned a plot of land in the section belonging to Reb Simchah, which was bequeathed to his heirs after his death. Reb Simchah had stipulated that this plot should not be sold for any price in years to come; instead, the Trust was to wait and see how his heirs would treat the synagogue. It was Reb Simchah who had, forty years ago, planned this brilliant tactic — the opposition of C. M. to any sort of construction on the plot, as well as the hiding of the riddles, copies of which are in our possession and would have been sent to you had you not found them."

Waving the copies in the air, the chairman continued: "Reb Simchah authorized us to add to or change the riddle according to the circumstances. To our delight, this was unnecessary, because the names he originally used are still perfectly suited to the present situation.

"Now you are here," the chairman added. "In accordance with Reb Simcha's plan of forty years ago, we must present his heirs with the following choice: C. M. will withdraw its opposition to the construction project on the condition that Reb Simcha's heirs erect a Torah center on the plot of land under discussion. It must include a well-appointed synagogue, an Orthodox elementary school, and a yeshivah. The heirs must invest fifteen million dollars in this project, with the remainder to be covered by C. M. Before you are precise blueprints of the structures which Reb Simchah planned."

The chairman's monotone was cut short by Reb Tuvia. "But why did Reb Simchah send us on this long journey?" he asked in amazement. "Had you sent Josh a detailed letter with all these conditions, he would have agreed to them." Tuvia turned to glance at Josh. "Isn't that so?"

Josh rose. A hush descended on the room.

"You are mistaken if you think that my grandfather's main purpose in founding the C. M. company was the perpetuation of the synagogue. Were that so, he could merely have deposited ten million dollars in a fund in its name. My grandfather established the company for *my* sake.

"My grandfather saw how his son was veering away from him and from religion, and understood that his grandson would not see himself as a Jew at all, as has indeed occurred. My grandfather had the sense way back then to plant the seeds wnich took root in my heart. For a number of years, until I reached the age of eight, he would sit at my bedside and sing me a song — one song only. Although I didn't understand the words, I loved its haunting melody, and would along even without understanding the meaning of the words.

"My grandfather wanted me to return to the roots he had planted within me, and for that reason concocted this ingenious plan which would culminate in my finding myself, and which would bring me face to face with an elderly Jew named Reb Yeedle Cohen.

"Don't you see? That Jew, the suffering on his face, the longing in his voice, is the living embodiment of the Jewish people. Suddenly I see how, despite myself, I am returning and reconnecting to my childhood, to that same people from which I tried to distance myself.

"Perpetuating and rebuilding the synagogue was not my grandfather's only goal," Josh continued, his voice laden with emotion. "He not only wanted the synagogue to be rebuilt by me, with my money — he wanted me to *want* to rebuild it.

"Do you understand?" sobbed Josh. "Forty years ago, when he sat beside my bed, he envisioned me in *Eretz Yisrael*, standing on a balcony in Batei Hungarin. He saw my overflowing heart, he saw the seeds he had planted in me suddenly putting forth shoots. It's beyond my comprehension. Did he know how I would agonize over the changes occurring within me? Why did he choose to torment my already tortured soul? Tell me, what should I do now?"

Those present sat motionless.

Josh continued. " 'Pay heed to the soul' — now I understand the meaning of these words. I have never paid heed to my soul. Perhaps I was afraid. I am, believe me, afraid for my soul. I was always afraid. Do you understand?

"What have you done to me, Zeidy? Why did you do this to me, Zeidy? I loved you so much."

A deathly silence blanketed the room. Those present stared at the impassioned Josh as if he had placed on the table, alongside his raging soul, his broken heart. They dared not speak.

"What did you do to me, Zeidy?" wept Josh. "Why did you leave me? Why did you stop singing the beautiful song? Why did you leave a sensitive soul alone in this cruel world? Why?"

Josh remained in Israel one more week. He wanted to hear Reb Yeedle once more — walking through the alleyways singing. He did, but this time it was with a small yarmulke on his head.

The following Sunday, Josh returned to the United States, along with Reb Tuvia. This time, the flight was more relaxed. The amazing two weeks they had spent together had left them close friends.

ೋ Postscript

Five years later in a dedication ceremony, a dignified-looking man affixed a mezuzah on the door of the luxurious Beth Aharon Synagogue. When he had completed his task, an announcement was heard: "We thank our great benefactor, a man of true generosity, a man who regularly sets aside time for Torah study, Mr. Yehoshua Zilberstein, for his important donation of fifty million dollars to our institution. We invite our guests to join us for the dinner."

The guests found their places, and the orchestra began to play a plaintive melody. The gazes of Reb Tuvia and Yehoshua met. The singer took the microphone and began to sing: "Pay heed to the soul. . . "

The Alterer

It was the saddest Shavuos night Yoel Dinker had ever spent in his whole life. And he, who had known many sad nights, even without their being connected to Shavuos, sat chilled — and, for the first time, felt frightened.

Most likely it was that night when his inner defense mechanism broke down, a night when the thick skin of indifference, so to speak, which enveloped him and had only grown thicker over the years, sloughed off. Yoel Dinker was afraid.

Yoel was the top student in the yeshivah. The problem was that he had held that position for fifteen years. He had entered the yeshivah when he was seventeen, armed with numerous recommendations. High hopes were pinned on him, and he did not disappoint. He fulfilled each and every one of them, and even exceeded them.

Soon enough, the other students came over to talk with him in learning, to benefit from his vast knowledge and exceptional depth of thought. They admired him and treated him with respect.

Not many years passed before he became the most authoritative student in the yeshivah. Everyone came over to him, not only to hear him explain the *sugyah* but to ask him for advice and to study his approach to learning Torah. All saw him as someone knowledgeable, learned and intelligent, a person with whom to consult and to whom to listen.

The years passed. His friends married. The younger students who took their places looked at him with admiring eyes, for they saw for themselves his wisdom and scholarly acumen, and that his fear of Heaven preceded his wisdom. He, though, remained a yeshivah *bachur*. He never married. Often, he would ask himself why. He had never thought of himself as especially choosy. He never refused to listen to offers. Of those that did come his way, though, there was always something that prevented them from continuing, and they never reached final stages.

He had long ago come to the definite conclusion that he had nothing to do with the delay in finding his mate. He repeatedly went over in his mind the memories of the many offers proposed to him over the years. He knew clearly that those he had rejected were truly not suitable for him, and that some of those who rejected him were suitable but for some strange reason did not want him.

What's the point in thinking about it? They were all already married anyway and had families. What point is there in crying over spilt milk? It would break his heart. He always kept himself from such thoughts. But not tonight. Something inside him began to gnaw at him. Feelings of depression welled up in his heart.

He looked around. Yes. He was familiar with the faces of the young *bachurim* who studied alongside him. They respected him, and even approached him in learning, often asking him to clarify their questions. And he didn't disappoint them. However, over the years, things seemed to have changed. He didn't know how it had happened. Maybe the gap in age. They no longer discussed their problems with him, no longer consulted with him about how best to act, as had most of the *bachurim* in the past. Yoel Dinker tried to recall the last time someone had come over to him with a question like that. It must have been years. He hadn't even noticed how the wall had formed between him and them, a natural wall.

Yoel looked around and was startled to see himself surrounded by children. He was nearly twice as old as they were. He didn't know most of them, didn't come to converse with them, didn't join in their conversations on the subjects that interested them. In the dining room, there were few he would sit with, and he scorned their youthful laughter. He was sure it was simply the spiritual decline of the generations, *yeridas hadoros*. But now, the thought occurred to him that it was he who was becoming more distant and not they who had declined.

His fear grew tangible. Yoel suddenly felt alone. He had been sitting in the same place for fifteen years and no one really knew him. There was no one he could talk to. Everyone treated him with the respect they would give... their grandfather. He was alone.

Yoel remembered that many years before, he too had sat in the dining room dispelling the cloud of seriousness, and had talked about this and that with friends his age. He began to recall their names and faces. Tall Yisrael, Yochanan the son of the *dayan*, Itzik, with whom he had liked to argue, Yosef, Chaim, and Efraim... Efraim "Potscher."

"*Boker tov* Efraim," they had called him.

What a likable boy he had been!

Suddenly he remembered, and the smile which had begun to turn up the corners of his mouth, faded. An incident connected to Efraim surfaced in his memory. It was

Shavuos about — was it ten years ago? Or perhaps even twelve?

Yoel didn't feel well. He closed his Gemara, slowly left the *beis midrash*, and went up to his room in the empty dorm. Everyone else was in the *beis midrash* that night. He sat on his bed and flipped through his memories of those distant times. Oh, how far away they were, those days when he had still been a young boy, happy and surrounded by friends...

❑ ❑ ❑

Everyone called him "Efraim Potscher" (Efraim the hitter). But it should be noted that Efraim never hit a living soul, not even an animal, except for the strong "hits" one hand gave to the other each morning for many years.

Efraim was the yeshivah's waker-upper. Every day he would get up an hour early, make his preparations, take a good look at his watch and, exactly half an hour before *davening*, would begin clapping his hands as he walked the halls of the yeshivah.

No matter how you looked at Efraim Potscher you saw a huge pair of hands, somehow connected to broad, thick shoulders. In general, Efraim Potscher was considered a creation too thick and broad, even without taking into consideration his famous broad smile, and it was certainly hard to think of Efraim Potscher without the broad smile usually covering his face from one ear to the other and as much as possible, close to both of them.

Efraim Potscher used to cover himself in clothes far too worn, and it seemed that he opposed, in principle, that device called an iron. He certainly never paid attention to minor details like tucking in his shirt or arranging his tzitzis, thus giving them plenty of room to breathe.

Nonetheless, Efraim Potscher was never thought of as a "strange" *bachur*. The opposite was true. It was as if there had never been a *bachur* as popular and accepted as Efraim Potscher in the history of the yeshivah. The fact that he was equipped with a thicker build than usual and the fact that he covered it in rags did not diminish his stature in the eyes of the *bachurim*. To a certain degree, it could be said, "the opposite."

The interesting appearance of Efraim Potscher and his no less interesting job turned him into an address which could not be passed by unnoticed. Whenever he passed through the halls, there was always someone who would clap him on his broad shoulders and say the usual greeting, "*Boker tov*, Efraim" — even if it was already afternoon, night, or any other hour.

All this, plus the many deeds of *chesed* he used to do, turned him into the most popular *bachur* in the yeshivah, as happens in every yeshivah to boys of his type. But because he turned into a "public institution" no one ever bothered to ask him about his feelings, problems, aspirations or fears. Probably everyone thought that he didn't have a lot, or even a few.

There was one day of the year when Efraim stood out more than any other day. The morning after Shavuos night.

With the *bachurim* still tired and exhausted from their night of studying with no sleep, there arose, as it did each year, the problem of *birkas hashachar*, for only someone who has slept is allowed to say those blessings, while the others have to make due with saying amen.

Usually, the *bachurim* searched through the rooms looking for someone whose tiredness had overcome him to the point where he had fallen asleep. Usually, the one who said the blessing would feel that his task was far from an honor, for everyone knew that if he had studied that night, it had only been in a dream.

During the years Efraim Potscher studied in the yeshivah it was he whom they woke up from sleep to say *birkas hashachar*.

Efraim would wash his face, put on his clothes, and appear in the *beis midrash*, along with his generous smile and the remnants of sleep still quite evident. Then, with a broad sweep of his arms, he would wrap himself in a tallis, smile in all directions as if he had won first prize in some contest, approach the *amud*, and begin to sing out *birkas hashachar* as if it were the greatest honor of his life.

One year, the one Yoel Dinker remembered more than any other, he stood and watched Efraim wrap himself in the tallis in the center of a circle of young *bachurim*, when one of them said affectionately to him, "Tell me, Efraim, were you so engrossed in your learning that you didn't even notice the spider weaving its web on you?"

"Efraim," another asked, "what did you dream last night?"

These remarks were made with the full knowledge that Efraim would not be offended. And he wasn't, so everyone accepted it — except for Yoel. He face expressed a mixture of sorrow, compassion, and anger. *How does he let himself be made a fool of?* he asked himself.

And after prayers...Yes, he remembered it well. They sat in the dining room eating, tasting the cheesecakes. Suddenly, Yoel heard Iztik Sont laughingly ask Efraim, "What will you do after you get married? Who will give you the 'great honor' you get here?"

Yoel remembered listening carefully for Efraim's reply, which came with a laugh. "Don't worry. Wherever you go, the one who recites *birkas hashachar* gets this great 'honor.' I just hope that I'll find a wife who will agree to endure this honor too. She'll have to be a real *tzaddekes*."

Everyone laughed. Everyone but Yoel. It was beyond his understanding how his fellow tablemate could continually make so light of his self-esteem. "Tell me, do you think someone will agree to marry you?" The cold voice of Yoel sounded like the crack of a whip.

Absolute silence. Everyone but Efraim saw that Yoel was not joking.

"Ha," laughed Efraim. "Someone will fall into the trap, don't worry."

"I don't understand what's so funny," Yoel lashed out again. "Do you think anyone would agree to marry someone like you?"

Efraim fell silent. He looked at Yoel and suddenly realized that he wasn't joking. His smile disappeared. His face turned red. His lips moved as if he wanted to speak but no sound came out.

"Stop making a fool out of yourself," cried Yoel. "It's not fitting for you. No one will take..."

❑ ❑ ❑

The voices seemed to be mocking him from the distant past, surging straight into Yoel's dark room. More than ten years had passed. He broke out into a cold sweat. He remembered how his friends had silenced him, how he had ignored their requests to stop hurting Efraim's feelings, and how he had raged at Efraim, who stood there confused, forlorn and disgraced. Suddenly Yoel knew why his finding a mate had been delayed from On High. All of a sudden he realized that this was Hashem's way of signaling him that he had committed a serious misdeed. It had never even occurred to him to regret it. Why had he done it? How could he offend and embarrass a friend? He had never acted that way. Had it been his tiredness that night which had made him do it? Had he really raged against his good friend for a moment's foolishness?

Yoel lay down on his bed, his heart threatening to burst. Twelve years of suffering hadn't been enough of a price to pay. He knew all too well that Efraim had been happily married for the past ten years and that he had six children. He had met him a number of times. They had talked like old friends. It was obvious he had forgotten the incident, just as Yoel had. But Above it had not been forgotten.

The darkness outside grew thicker. A hot wind blew in through the window, hitting the face of a lonely, despairing man. Bitter scenes flashed across his mind. Sorrow overwhelmed his soul, causing a tempest of feelings and fears. He felt hollow, empty, as if there was nothing left for him. His success and his studies disappeared. Now he was just plain old Yoel Dinker, a *bachur* of thirty-two, whose fate no one was interested in. *I could stay in my room for a year and no one would notice*, he thought bitterly.

Thus he fell asleep.

❑ ❑ ❑

He awakened to a smiling face. A sunbeam informed him that it was morning and that he, Yoel Dinker, had spent Shavuos night sleeping. His room was filled with happy, animated *bachurim*. At long last they had found someone who could recite *birkas hashachar* for them. "Get up, Yoel. Come on, get up," they said.

He noticed that he had fallen asleep in his clothes, which now looked like wrinkled rags. His white shirt resembled a tablecloth which someone had rolled up and thrown into a laundry hamper. "*Nu*, hurry up. We need a chazan who can recite *birkas hashachar* for us."

Tired and confused, he washed his hands. He had barely managed to wash his face, when he was pushed along by dozens of *bachurim*, who burst out singing the customary Shavuos song: *"U'va'u chulam bi'vris yachad, na'aseh v'nishma amru k'echad. . ."*

They pulled him into the *beis midrash*, where hundreds of *bachurim* awaited him. *Ramim, roshei yeshivah* and *mashgichim* stood beside the eastern wall. They all looked at him with joy and satisfaction. Encouraging claps on his back accompanied his way forward. No one imagined what he was going through inside. It was their way of expressing their admiration for him. In their own way, they loved the aging bachelor, "the *alterer*" who sat beside them studying from morning till night, apart from them and not involved in their lives, yet answering their questions patiently. The fact that he had slept the entire Shavuos night did not diminish his stature. They knew that on many other nights he had remained awake studying. "Most likely," they said, "he felt weak."

Everyone thought that way. But thoughts cannot be seen. Yoel understood the exact opposite, just as he had understood it eleven years earlier. For Yoel, it was the most humiliating experience ever.

He forced a smile. Then, with a broad sweep of his arms, he wrapped himself in a tallis and began to recite *birkas hashachar*. Suddenly, the letters of his *siddur* blurred. He imagined himself standing trial, the cries of "amen" from the crowd seemed to him like the scornful cries of a mob who had already decided his fate.

The letters began to dance, his voice wavered. His eyes suddenly lost their focus.

He fainted.

Confusion reigned. Cups of water were splashed on him. From the fog, he felt them carry him to his room. A student remained to watch him. It took him a while to come back to himself, and when he at last he came to, he remembered everything. He buried his head in his hands and began to sob for the first time since he had been a child.

After prayers, many of the *bachurim* came in to see how he was feeling. But he only asked them apologetically to call the *mashgiach*.

He came, an elderly and distinguished man. Despite the years which had passed, the two had never held exceptionally long or deep conversations. But Yoel had always sensed that the *mashgiach* knew him better than he knew himself.

The door closed, and Yoel began to tell the *mashgiach* the story, which he now remembered so clearly, of what had happened eleven years ago.

When he finished his story, the *mashgiach* looked at him for a long time before answering. "There is something to it. I know you are incapable of hurting anyone. I know that this incident, which I am hearing about for the first time, was an isolated incident and was well meant. However," continued the *mashgiach*, "the error is a weighty one. I can't tell you why, because I promised not to. Exactly about what you hurt his feelings...*nu*, I can't say. My suggestion to you is this. On *motza'ei* Shavuos, find Efraim and apologize. That is all. I am certain he will forgive you, if he even remembers the incident. Most probably he doesn't remember. Otherwise he would have forgiven you in his heart long ago."

❏ ❏ ❏

The holiday ended late. Yoel found out Efraim's address. He lived in a distant city, but Yoel decided not to postpone his trip. The matter was eating him up.

He arrived there at midnight, praying he would find Efraim awake. He headed toward his house. A light was on. He knocked softly on the door. A small child opened it.

"Is your father home?" he asked.

"No."

"Where is he?"

"I don't know."

"Can you ask your mother?"

The child disappeared and returned a moment later. "He's learning," he said.

"Where?"

"I don't know."

Yoel thanked him, went down the stairs, and began to search the shuls.

He walked around for an hour. The shuls were closed. The people he met on the street shook their heads. It wasn't a city that was filled with shuls, certainly not the kind which remained open after midnight.

In the end, he reached a small out-of-the-way shul. A weak light shone from inside. He went in quietly and heard the singsong chant of someone learning. He slowly drew closer until he stood next to the lone learner, who was not even aware of his existence.

Efraim.

He stood and watched him for some time, afraid to disturb. All at once, he understood everything.

Suddenly he understood the enigmatic words of the *mashgiach*: "Exactly about what you hurt his feelings..." Yoel's understanding mind did not disappoint. Suddenly he realized that for years Efraim would go to sleep on Shavuos night and stay awake on *motza'ei* Shavuos. It was obvious. Here it was 1:30 A.M., and Efraim was still sitting and learning. *Why would he do it?* Yoel asked himself without coming up with any answers.

Thus he stood for quite a while, until he decided to take a *sefer* and sit down to learn, too. This act made a slight noise and suddenly a voice was heard. "Reb Yoel, what are you doing here?"

"I came to speak with you but... I don't want to disturb your learning."

"If you have come specially at an hour like this and have even found me here, it must be something important. It's a mitzvah to listen to a *talmid chacham* of your stature."

Efraim rose, prepared a cup of tea, and asked casually. "*Nu*, Reb Yoel, where do you live today?"

"In the yeshivah!"

"In the yeshivah? What, did you become a *ram*? How did you choose —"

"I'm still a *bachur*, Efraim. I'm not married. I still study in the yeshivah."

Efraim had no words… and didn't need any. His shocked expression said it all.

"Efraim, I'm certain that the fact that I still haven't found a wife is connected to you," said Yoel, and he told Efraim about that incident of eleven years ago. At first Efraim didn't remember a thing but slowly, as Yoel reminded him of all the details, he remembered.

Yoel finished his story and pleaded with Efraim to forgive him. He even mentioned the words of the *mashgiach* according to which it had been a grave error. "Now I know what that error was. I never imagined that you remained awake all night on *motza'ei* Shavuos. Your intention is probably to make sure that the voice of Torah will be heard the night after Shavuos night, when everyone else is tired. Isn't that it?"

❏ ❏ ❏

Efraim did not reply. He sat deep in thought, slightly sad. All of a sudden he began to speak, as if to himself. Yoel listened to his words and couldn't believe his ears.

"Master of the Universe," cried Efraim, "Who scrutinizes hearts and minds! You know that I was not angry at Yoel for hurting my feelings, and that soon afterwards I forgot about it completely. A Jew who toils over

Torah day and night stumbled over one transgression. For so many years afterwards he is stricken with suffering and sadness for that same transgression he unwittingly committed. Is it possible?

"The Master of the Universe knows that Yoel is a servant of Hashem and a great Torah scholar," Efraim said passionately, "yet he has one flaw in his character. Does he deserve to be punished for it? Proof of this flaw is that although he knows that I remain awake on the night after Shavuos instead of on Shavuos night, it doesn't occur to him why." Yoel understood all too well that Efraim words were really meant for him, so he listened intently. He wanted to know which flaw Efraim was talking about.

Efraim continued. "He thinks that my reason for remaining awake all night is related to Torah study. This is so because the world of Torah is his entire world. His mind is replete with Torah learning; his body, filled with mitzvos. But what about his heart? What covers it? Why is his mind open and his heart closed? Why doesn't he consider that there might be a completely different reason for my staying awake that night? If only some of the vast amount of Torah in his mind would penetrate his heart he would be worthy of being called a *gadol b'Yisrael*, and would even be worthy of guiding students. Now, he can't even marry — for an understanding heart is essential for married life. It's not enough to have an overflowing mind..."

Suddenly, Yoel understood that Heaven had dealt kindly with him by preventing him from marrying until then. He knew suddenly that he had never been mature enough for married life, because he hadn't truly understood its meaning well enough. He was flawed, with an indiscernible flaw whose power to damage and destroy nonetheless existed. Yoel felt a transformation taking place within his heart and soul. For the first time in his life, he *felt* — not only understood — what was happening.

Efraim sat down next to him. "Calm down, Yoel. I feel that everything will change from now on. You have to be happy. How can I make you happy? I know — I'll learn together with you *b'chavrusa*. I'll be happy and so will you. But what am I rambling on about? You've been awake since last night. Go to sle—"

"No, Efraim. I slept all last night."

"What?"

Yoel told Efraim what had happened to him on Shavuos night. He saw Efraim smile, then try hard to keep from laughing, and in the end, give in, taking Yoel along with him. All of a sudden the two of them were both laughing and crying, and Yoel felt that a heavy weight had been lifted from him.

❑ ❑ ❑

The two sat and learned for hour upon hour. The morning stars faded, and the sun's gentle rays began to penetrate the shul.

All of a sudden, the door opened. An old man entered. "That's the rabbi of the shul, the *av beis din* of the city," Efraim said to Yoel as he rose to prepare another cup of tea.

When he returned, he found Yoel engrossed in his thoughts, a broad smile on his face.

"Would you like to share your thoughts?" asked Efraim.

"I know why you stay awake on the night after Shavuos instead of on Shavuos night," Yoel said.

"Why?" Efraim asked, an eager look of expectancy on his face, hoping that Yoel really knew.

"It's because you know how badly the person who has to recite *birkas hashachar* the following morning feels, and you want to spare others that feeling. I'm positive."

A broad smile spread over Efraim's face. "No one knows about it except for the *mashgiach*, who 'caught' me one *motza'ei* Shavuos. He promised never to tell, and kept his word. But this time, I'm happy to reveal the secret."

"Why?" asked Yoel.

"Because now I know that a small opening has opened in your heart. You are not the same Yoel, who knows how to think but doesn't know how to feel. Now your flaw has been repaired. My prayer has been answered, and now all that's left is the matter of finding a mate."

They continued to study joyfully and enthusiastically until dawn, and without their even noticing it, a few worshipers appeared in shul. The two lifted their heads from the Gemara and met the penetrating eyes of the *rav*. Apparently, he had been watching them for a long time, without their being aware of it.

Suddenly, the *rav* motioned to Efraim, who went over to him.

"Who is your study partner?" he asked.

Efraim told him.

"Is he married?"

Efraim answered in the negative.

"I was watching him while he learned with you. He made a very favorable impression on me. I have a granddaughter. . . ." the *rav* sighed. "Although she is a bit older, she is the daughter of my son-in-law, a *rosh yeshivah*. What do you think? About his learning you don't have to say a thing. I saw and heard for myself. But aside from knowing how to learn, there are other things as well. I decided to check with you, since you certainly know him quite well. Please tell me. Knowledge, I saw that he has — he knows entire tractates — but what about his heart? What about his character, his *middos*? Tell me, does a feeling, sensitive Jewish heart beat within him?"

Ozer Dalim

Yussel Shailover marched down the street in a rush. He was hurrying to an important business meeting, a deal that was supposed to add a hefty amount of cash to his pockets. And there was nothing like the prospect of earning one sum or another to cause Yussel Shailover to hurry along his way.

Shailover was a successful businessman. Everyone admired his cool levelheadedness and the fact that he never allowed personal considerations to affect his business decisions. Shailover would never buy a product just because he liked the seller. That was because Shailover liked the money he put in his pocket better than anything. Other than that, there was no consideration in the world which would influence him.

The person who caused Yussel Shailover to slow his steps and even stop them completely was a fellow standing on the street corner who, armed with an old violin, was taking revenge on the well-known melody he was playing.

The innocent citizens walking by passed quickly because the tones which emanated from the fellow's violin were like the screams of an innocent lamb being taken to slaughter, except that chances were that the lamb wouldn't ask to be paid for his concert.

Truth be told, the hatted musician standing on the street corner did not demand a fee. His open violin case did that for him. However, very few people expressed their gratitude for his atrocious playing by tossing coins into the case. Those few who did, revealed their true opinions about his musical talents by means of the sour looks on their faces.

After he had completed his rendition of the well-known melody he was playing, the musician began to grate out a new composition. In a certain way, Yussel Shailover noted to himself that the poor man could, in a way, be called an "artist," for when it came to destroying a musical composition, it would be hard to find anyone like him. Yussel mused that they should pass a special law against people maiming compositions that weren't their own.

Soon enough, Yussel Shailover was given to realize that it had been a mistake to stand there facing the fellow with the squeaky violin, because there was a great chance that he was about to recruit him into his circle of fans, the number of whom was no greater than the number of coins he had collected in his case.

However, before Yussel could manage to flee, the violinist — without stopping his sawing for a moment — called out to Yussel, "Please sit down on the bench. I can see that my playing interests you. In that case, wait a little while longer, and I'll play my masterpiece."

Yussel tried to say something about an important meeting which he had to attend, but there is nothing like the sound of sawing to nip a declamation in the bud. In no time at all, the violinist stood opposite the bench Yussel was sitting on, his eyes closed, playing.

Yussel was forced to admit to himself that this composition was much more horrifying than the previous ones. He dared not hint such a thing to the violinist, of course, lest he try to improve his playing in Yussel's presence.

So as not to waste his time, Yussel tried to recognize among the broken squeaks of the violin the original tune the violinist was trying to play. After a great deal of effort, it came to him, and he discovered that it was the melody used by the chazan who was honored with the sixth *hakafah* on Simchas Torah.

"*Ozer dalim hoshiyah na*," the man cried out along with the violin. To his dismay, Yussel discovered that there was a great similarity between the violin and the man in whose hands it was captive. They both displayed a great deal of animosity towards the original melody and played it completely off tune.

The man finished playing, bowed in all directions, and then sat down beside Yussel. "Do you know why I play that way? Do you think I have time on my hands? Wait a while and I'll tell you why I need the coins which passersby occasionally toss my way."

A lot of choices Yussel didn't have. He had already missed his important meeting. Therefore, he fixed his gaze on the old man, who began to tell his story.

❑ ❑ ❑

Shimik Blecher had grown up in a very poor home. His father, Kalman, a porter at the docks, found it hard to support his family. Shimik had so many brothers and sisters that the house could barely contain them all.

No matter when you looked at him, Shimik was always busy thinking and planning his future. Actually, people considered Shimik considered a dreamer, which did not particularly please his father, for there was no future for a dreamer amongst the blue-collar workers who lived in Shimik's neighborhood.

In Shimik's father's opinion, the right to think and imagine was the province of the wealthy, who did not have to seek their daily bread, something that could certainly not be said about Shimik and others of his social class.

Shimik's thoughts raced ahead, nonetheless. He dreamed about how he'd make a few profitable deals and become rich; he dreamed of how he'd buy new and expensive clothes for his brothers and sisters; he dreamed of how he'd buy his family a new home; and he envisioned the ceremony installing the *sefer Torah* he'd buy with part of his fortune.

Shimik's fondest dream was to purchase the title of *Chasan Torah* for his father, Kalman. This dream would flood Shimik's mind every Simchas Torah as he watched the sale of the various honors in his shul — an *aliyah* to the Torah, leading the various *hakafos*, reading the *maftir*, or becoming *Chasan Bereshis* and *Chasan Torah*. At such times, Shimik would look at his father, whose gaze would wander back and forth from the wealthy Lipa Shleifer to Netta Gold the *gabbai* who were competing for the honor of *Chasan Torah*. Then and there, Shimik decided that the following year he would purchase *Chasan Torah* and give it to his father. And that was final!

Once, during a reckless moment, Shimik revealed some of his thoughts to one of his brothers, and with that, his life became miserable. They all laughed and ridiculed him. "Shimik the millionaire," they called him, a nickname which soon spread among all the children of the neighborhood.

This nickname, and the derision it elicited, did not do much to increase Shimik's acceptance among his peers and actually distanced him to the extent that he could always be seen wandering around alone, speaking to no one, not even to himself, engrossed in his thoughts and plans.

A year passed, and Simchas Torah arrived once more. Gold and Shleifer were in the midst of vying with one another. The price of *Chasan Torah* skyrocketed to four thousand lirot. Shimik discovered that he didn't have the ready cash to put in a bid which would outdo the two of them, as he had originally planned. Actually, Shimik wondered what he would do with the twenty agurot he had managed to amass over the year.

The selling of the *aliyahs* and the *hakafos* had nearly ended, save for one *hakafah* which had no buyer — the sixth *hakafah*, during which the chazan cries out: "*Ozer dalim hoshiyah na* — He Who helps the poor, save us." Apparently there was no congregant prepared to donate even half a cracked lira to publicly cry out, "*Ozer dalim hoshiyah na.*" As a result, every year when the *gabbai* announced the sale of this *hakafah*, the congregants would begin to whisper to each other about all sorts of things, and the *hakafah* would remain unsold.

And so, when it came time for the sixth *hakafah*, the *gabbai*, Netta Gold, would scan the congregation for someone who would be willing to carry the burden of *Ozer Dalim*. Not finding anyone like that, his eyes would suddenly light up and he would cry out: "Reb Kalman Blecher is honored with *Ozer Dalim*."

Shimik gazed first at the *gabbai*, then at his father, and back to the *gabbai* again. He saw the *gabbai* and some of his friends laughing at the very idea. Even his father laughed. Only Shimik understood the meaning of that laughter. Shimik wanted to shout. He wanted to cry. He wanted to shake the *gabbai* with all his might. But he did none of those things. He merely looked with glazed eyes at his father who sadly forced himself to accept the honor and lead the congregation in *Ozer Dalim*.

Shimik barely heard the words his father sang. He looked at his brothers, who were laughing heartily. He couldn't understand how they could laugh. He knew and felt his father's pain. Couldn't they see it? Didn't they understand? He knew his way of thinking was unlike theirs — but to such a degree?

The *hakafah* ended, and with it all the *hakafos*. Shimik didn't dance; he didn't sing. He looked at Netta the *gabbai* who had finally won the title of *Chasan Torah* after having offered five thousand lirot for it, and had thus vanquished Shleifer the *gvir* who was forced to be content with *Chasan Bereshis*, for only forty-five hundred lirot. Shimik asked himself, *Was that what my teacher meant when he sang, "Chaim she'tehe banu ahavas Torah — a life in which we will be imbued with love of Torah"?* Shimik couldn't think of an answer.

All of a sudden, another goal was added to Shimik's list. His original way of thinking had given rise to an idea, which, in his opinion, would wipe out his father's disgrace and transform it into great honor.

❧ *Twenty Years Later*

Shimik was now twenty-eight. Only after much effort had a *shidduch* been found for him, for he was neither good-looking nor impressive. Neither was he much of a scholar, and in fact, was rather far from it. Years of worry had passed for his father, Kalman, seeing his son still unmarried. Kalman admired his son for not leaving the yeshivah. Truth be told, even though Shimik's friends in yeshivah viewed him as a bit strange, he had still found his place among them.

That was because he was very helpful to them and to the yeshivah's staff, thanks to his brainstorms.

In ways known only to him, he would get special discounts for suits, hats, and other items of clothing for his fellow yeshivah students. To the administrators he would suggest inexpensive yet effective ways of soliciting funds. Upon his suggestion, the neglected entrance to the yeshivah was transformed into a reception room, which impressed visitors and opened their hearts. Shimik developed an idea for a way to heat water in the winter, an idea which saved the yeshivah a lot of money and was copied by other yeshivos. He instituted a new kind of raffle, somehow got people to donate many costly prizes, took care of getting the right publicity all over the country, managed to spread a network of representatives to sell tickets everywhere, and paid off all the debts of the yeshivah.

Even though Shimik tried to maintain set study schedules and to abide by all of the *rosh yeshivah*'s attendance rules, he knew quite well that he could be called an "activist." He had overheard a certain conversation which took place between his father and the *rosh yeshivah*. Although Shimik knew he was different, it was still important to him to fit in as much as possible.

At last he found a suitable marriage partner. Shimik got a girl as ordinary as he was, and, accompanied by the worries and concern of his parents and friends, he set out in life.

❏ ❏ ❏

When Simchas Torah came around that year, Shimik went to his father's shul, as he had for the past twenty years. *Ozer Dalim* had always been given to one of the ordinary men, the shul members deemed less important. It was as if it were some kind of disgrace for a more distinguished member to buy it.

That year, Shimik decided to fulfill his dream of twenty years before.

The first five *hakafos* were sold, and the turn of the sixth arrived. As a matter of routine, the long-standing *gabbai* Netta Gold announced the sale of the sixth *hakafah*, and even quoted a beginning price, which was never paid anyway.

"Fifty! Going once, going twice —"

"One hundred," Shimik's voice was heard.

Everyone's eyes turned to him.

"One hundred?" laughed the *gabbai*. "Wake up, Shimik. It's *Ozer Dalim*."

"One hundred," repeated Shimik.

"Two hundred and fifty," said Gold, curious to see Shimik's reaction.

"Five hundred," Shimik responded without hesitation.

The congregation was in an uproar. Such a thing was unheard of. Someone was willing to pay more for *Ozer Dalim* than for any other *hakafah*?

Gold tried to test Shimik's seriousness once again. He dropped out when the price reached a thousand lirot.

When the fifth *hakafah* had ended, Shimik was called upon to lead *Ozer Dalim*, and raised his voice in song. Although Shimik was far from being a chazan, and was casually making a basic change in the customary *minhag*, no one paid any attention to that because they were too busy watching the amazing scene unfold before their eyes.

After the holiday, Shimik returned home, and soon enough news of his success in the business world became common knowledge. Some of his ideas for watering systems and energy saving devices were sold to large firms abroad, for generous sums. It was hard for the shul members not to recall over and over again what had occurred in their small shul.

The next year, when Gold the *gabbai* came to sell *Ozer Dalim* he again tried to buy it for himself. This time, though, he wasn't alone. Others also displayed an interest in that same *hakafah*. Unknown someones linked Shimik's sudden turn of fortune to his purchase of *Ozer Dalim* the previous year. Shimik's remark that their surmise was probably valid caused the worshipers to compete fiercely for this choice *hakafah*. In the end, there remained three in the bidding: Gold the *gabbai*, Shleifer the *gvir*... and Shimik.

The *hakafah*'s price skyrocketed. Never in the history of the shul had such prices been offered for a *hakafah*. When the bidding reached one thousand lirot, Shleifer the *gvir* dropped out. When it climbed to three thousand, Shimik was the one to get the *hakafah*.

When the sixth *hakafah* was announced, all looked in Shimik's direction. He, though, turned to the *gabbai* and whispered something in his ear. Gold nodded his head, and announced: "Reb Kalman *ben* Moshe is honored with *Ozer Dalim*."

Everyone gazed at Kalman with awe — including Shimik. What he saw brought him happiness, on the one hand, and depression on the other. Although Kalman was filled with joy and satisfaction, only Shimik could detect a trace of disapproval in his face.

Prayers ended, and all marveled over the fact that Kalman had been accorded the honor which the wealthiest and most respected men in the shul had vied for unsuccessfully. No one remembered that until then, receiving this *hakafah* had been considered a real humiliation.

Shimik and his father walked home in silence.

"Thank you," stated Kalman briefly. He opened his mouth as if to add something but changed his mind and said not a word.

Another year passed. News of Shimik's meteoric rise to riches continued to flow. He became known as a brilliant businessman, with everyone talking about his ingenious ideas and brainstorms which had brought him so much wealth.

The following year, a veritable battle took place in the shul. Everyone competed for the *hakafah*. People who for an entire year had put aside their money so that they would be able to buy it fell vanquished by Shimik's outrageous offers.

Once again Reb Kalman received the great honor, and again, as the pair walked home together, he stated a brief thank you. But this time, Kalman could not restrain himself.

"Do you know what, Shimik? You are filled with ideas. Ideas which fill me with amazement and leave me astounded that they are the product of my own son's mind — a son whose great mind I mistakenly underestimated. But of all your brilliant ideas, I am certain that this idea of raising the value of *Ozer Dalim* in so original and clever a way is the best one of them all. I am awed by this simple idea which testifies to your understanding of human nature.

"However, it seems to me that you have also become ensnared by your very own idea, somewhat like the old man who sent everyone to gather dates which were supposedly being given out for free, and in the end found himself running along with the crowd. I don't like this competition. It's not a competition for the honor of *Ozer Dalim* but rather for self-glorification. You have achieved your aim, Shimik. Be satisfied with that."

"What about the other *hakafos*, the various honors like *Chasan Torah*? Don't they contain an element of self-glorification, too?" asked Shimik.

Kalman thought a bit and said, "Perhaps you are right. My mind isn't as sharp as yours. However, that's my feeling. Leave things as they are, Shimik. You have done your share. *Ozer Dalim* is expensive enough, don't you agree?"

❧ Twenty Years Later

For twenty years Reb Kalman received the great honor of leading *Ozer Dalim*. Everyone respected him because of it, and even complimented him on having such a successful son. But Reb Kalman would respond to these compliments with a cold politeness which no one understood. Only his son Shimik understood, yet he could not muster the courage to stop his mad pursuit of honor.

With each passing year, Shimik noticed that his father was deriving less and less enjoyment from the honor. At a certain point, he saw that his father did not want it at all, and that he was accepting it only for the sake of his son's honor. After a few more years, Shimik began to perceive that each time his father was called up to lead the sixth *hakafah* of *Ozer Dalim*, he would suffer immensely. When the twentieth year arrived, Shimik looked at his father and saw what he had seen forty years ago when Reb Kalman had suffered the humiliation in front of the entire congregation, the humiliation that had given rise to Shimik's idea of transforming the *hakafah* into an unobtainable one.

Shimik's father was already over seventy years old. After the prayer service, the two walked back to the house in which Shimik had been born, the house which had been expanded and renovated with the help of his vast wealth.

The two walked side by side. Kalman didn't say a word. Neither did Shimik. The thoughts of both were racing.

"I don't feel well," Reb Kalman told his son. Shimik looked at his father and understood that this wasn't a routine complaint. Suddenly, he saw his father's head fall and his body falter. Shimik caught his father just in time and carried him home. On the way, he asked someone to call a doctor.

Once home, Shimik placed his father on his bed and removed his shoes. Shimik was terrified. He needed his father so much! He couldn't be without him.

"Look, Shimik — my strength is waning. I wanted to tell you, you were a good son to me, Shimik. I know how much you thought of me."

Shimik looked at his father and wondered what he meant. The old man continued.

"I know quite well when the idea about *Ozer Dalim* first came to you. In my mind's eye, I still see the shocked look on your face when the *gabbai* offended me. Yes, it was then that the spark was first ignited.

"Shimik, I want you to know that I deeply admired your devotion to the mitzvah of *kibbud av*. Yet I have never stopped regretting the fact that you weren't motivated by the need to honor *Ozer Dalim* but by your wanting to honor me. I don't know why I never told you this. Perhaps I was afraid to bring up the subject. But now that I am going the way of all men, I want to tell you one thing: You have done enough for my honor. Now you must think only about the honor of *Ozer Dalim*."

The old man's eyelids fluttered. "Come closer, Shimik, my son. I want to take leave of you. I love you so much. I had such great *nachas* from you."

Shimik bent closer to his father, who raised his head a bit and kissed the weeping Shimik on his forehead. The elderly man closed his eyes and returned his pure soul to his Maker.

❑ ❑ ❑

Seated on the bench, Yussel Shailover listened to the fascinating story of the elderly violinist. He did not have a moment's regret that he had met him and wanted to know what had happened in the end.

The old man did not disappoint him and continued his tale:

During the week of shiva, Shimik was far more withdrawn than any of his brothers. Guilt tortured him over his having caused his father such great anguish over so many years, and for having failed to understand the numerous hints sent his way, either through words or facial expressions. Shimik reached the conclusion that his father's assessment that he had not really been concerned about the honor of *Ozer Dalim* had been accurate. He resolved to fulfill his father's final request and think only about the honor of *Ozer Dalim*.

And what did Shimik do the next year if not exactly that?

He made a deal with one of the congregants, a man of great integrity, whom he trusted not to say a thing about Shimik's latest idea. Shimik authorized him to purchase the rights to *Ozer Dalim*, and to promise any sum demanded. Shimik suggested a ceiling price which was so high that it was inconceivable for anyone to outdo it. The agreement obligated the agent to bestow the right to lead the *hakafah* as he saw fit, save for the first year, when the buyer himself would merit it. Shimik didn't care who was selected for the honor. What mattered to him now was preserving *Ozer Dalim*'s honor... and that it would continue to be the most popular *hakafah* of the day and not an unwanted one, tossed to beggars.

Shimik's inspiration came to pass. Of course, during the first year, it was a surprise to see Shimik give up at quite an early stage in the bidding after having stubbornly insisted on purchasing the *hakafah* at all costs for so many years. There were those who explained this by saying that Shimik had only wanted to honor his father, and that for himself the privilege wasn't that important. Many saw this as an opportunity for them to try and secure the longed-for honor, and they rushed to pledge sizable sums. However, one of the shul's members, Shmuel Reinfeld by name, surpassed them all with his bid, and in the end bought *Ozer Dalim* for the highest price ever.

When Shmuel Reinfeld lifted his voice and sang, "*Ozer dalim hoshiyah na*," the congregants felt that a new chapter had opened in their lives, and that a long and remarkable epoch had ended.

Of course, none of them had the faintest idea that the large sum which Shmuel Reinfeld was paying to the community's coffers the day after Simchas Torah had been handed to him a few moment's prior to his appearance in the shul's office by Shimik Blecher.

Shimik too felt his heart twist. It wasn't easy for him to pay so large a sum without people knowing that he was the donor. It was precisely when that thought crossed his mind, though, that he understood how correct his father had been in his assessment that until then Shimik had been concerned only with the glory. Shimik gave the sum with a full heart, without any hesitations.

This happened the following year, too. Shmuel Reinfeld purchased the sought-after *hakafah* at the highest price and honored someone with it. Everyone was satisfied. Shimik was pleased that the honor of *Ozer Dalim* was preserved, and Shmuel Reinfeld didn't lose a thing from the deal.

❏ ❏ ❏

Then difficult times came upon Shimik. He wasn't growing any younger, and he no longer came up with in-

ventions and brilliant ideas as he had in the past. Shimik
realized all too late that he had acted hastily in not taking
the trouble to register patents for all his many inventions
over the years. Had he done so, he would have remained
wealthy his entire life. But now Shimik's funds were
dwindling.

Nonetheless, he continued to purchase *Ozer Dalim*.

At first, he did not notice that his savings were
dwindling. However, as time went by, Shimik began to
realize that he would have to lower his standard of living. He
did so without any great difficulty. He had already married
off his children well. He didn't want to become dependent
on them, nor did he want them to realize how bad his
financial situation was. They, in turn, knew absolutely
nothing about the heavy expense their father incurred every
year for *Ozer Dalim*. They thought that their father had
merely given up his custom of out-bidding everyone for the
sixth *hakafah*.

But he hadn't. Shimik lowered his standard of living,
sold the many works of art he had collected throughout his
life, and lived on that. Actually, if it weren't for the expensive
purchase he made every year in Tishrei, Shimik wouldn't
have had a moment's worry about providing for his basic
needs. Nonetheless, it never occurred to him to instruct
Reinfeld to lower his bid, even though, over the years,
Reinfeld had turned out to be very generous — at least when
it came to Shimik's money.

Then came the year when Shimik turned seventy.
Right after Simchas Torah of that year, he needed no accountant to discover that he didn't even have one thin dime,
except for a few thousand left in some bank account. Lack
of funds, in and of itself, didn't especially bother him; what
worried him was how he would purchase *Ozer Dalim* the
forthcoming year.

Shimik searched his large and empty house, and what did he find there if not a small violin which he had once purchased in Vienna?

At first Shimik tried to calculate how much he could get for the violin. As he did so, he tried to draw the violin's bow across the thin strings, and the tune which emerged from within gave him another brilliant idea — perhaps the last one in his life. *I'll go and play for people and with what they give me, I'll be able to purchase Ozer Dalim next year, too.*

❑ ❑ ❑

Night fell. Stars twinkled above. The streets were empty, and only two people could be seen — an elderly man wearing a worn suit, and a second man wearing an expensive, well-tailored one and carrying an attaché case. The elderly man licked his lips. The effort of speaking was hard for him.

"I've been standing on this corner for several months already," the elderly man said sadly to Yussel Shailover. "The truth is, people aren't that fond of my pieces. Perhaps because they're sad? Tell me the truth, isn't that so?"

Yussel thought a little. He ignored for the moment something undefined which was beginning to surface from the depths of his heart, and he answered according to what he had believed all his life.

"If you ask me, Mr. Shimik Blecher, I simply don't understand this appalling waste of yours each year," Yussel Shailover began. "Is it justified from a business standpoint? Is it an investment for the future? It seems to me that you've gotten some kind of crazy idea into your head. It's as if you want to waste your money. I can't understand anyone acting that way. Do you really think that *Ozer Dalim* needs the illusory honor you accord it? Do you really think that that is the way to honor it? I think that you should stop this ridiculous extravagance. It makes absolutely no sense."

Having given this speech, Yussel had nothing more to say. He removed a bill from his pocket, threw it into the violin case, and slowly disappeared into the darkness.

Shimik Blecher was left sitting alone on the bench astonished, confused, and embarrassed. This was the first time he had told his story to anyone who he had mistakenly thought was interested in his music. In hindsight, it seemed that he had met up with the coldest person on the face of the globe, if one could judge by his hurtful reaction.

Shimik Blecher lifted his violin and tried to play a melody. The wailing sound it emitted, though, frightened him. He packed up his violin and trudged back home, broken in spirit.

❑ ❑ ❑

Simchas Torah arrived. Moshe Gold the *gabbai*, the son of the deceased Netta Gold, began to sell the *hakafos*.

When he reached the sixth *hakafah* and announced the initial high price, all eyes turned towards Shmuel Reinfeld. He did not disappoint them and made a high bid. A number of congregants raised it, and he, in a monotone, raised it even higher. The price skyrocketed to unheard-of heights. Moshe Gold himself tried to raise the price, until it exceeded all bounds. Then he despaired. Reinfeld called out an astounding price: "Eight thousand." Gold lifted his hand to signal that he had given in. "Going once, going twice, going —"

"Nine thousand," a voice was heard from the last bench in the shul.

All eyes turned in the direction of the voice hoping to see who had made the offer, but a tallis hid the unknown bidder's face.

Shmuel Reinfeld recovered from the shock and raised the price too. The stranger didn't give in and continued to raise the price higher and higher.

Shimik sat in the first row and knew that the bids were nearing the ceiling price he had permitted Shmuel Reinfeld. He knew also that the price already offered would leave him in debt. However, he hoped to be able to pay it by next year. He brooded over the fact that precisely now, when it was so hard for him, some stranger had come along, like the work of Satan, and raised the price. Why did he deserve it?

Shmuel Reinfeld bid the top price Shimik had allowed him. He glanced in the direction of Shimik, who was planning to tell him he could raise the price a bit.

Then the stranger called out a higher price. Silence prevailed. Shimik saw the questioning gaze of Shmuel Reinfeld. Reb Moshe Gold cried out, "Going once..." *Decide quickly*, Reinfeld's eyes begged. "Going twice," called Moshe Gold, and suddenly Shimik realized that if he told Reinfeld to raise the bid, it would only be for the sake of his own honor, not *Ozer Dalim*'s. Well did Shimik recall his father's last request, and with a slight nod of his head indicated to Reinfeld to stop.

"Going thrice — it's his!" cried Reb Moshe Gold.

For the first time since Shimik had given him the job of buying *Ozer Dalim*, Shmuel Reinfeld was not so honored. The members of the shul felt that once more a page had been turned.

The *hakafos* began. Shimik tried to dance and rejoice. But instead, he danced and cried. He didn't know why he was crying but he couldn't stop dancing, either. An entire lifetime passed before his eyes, under the magnifying glass of *Ozer Dalim*. Had it all been worthwhile? Perhaps all people pass their lives under the magnifying glass they've chosen for themselves. Was it as important as *Ozer Dalim*?

Was his father crying, too, in Heaven, or perhaps actually laughing? When would he merit to be beside his father? He missed him. He would have preferred to have been under the magnifying glass of his father, Reb Kalman. For some reason, it seemed clearer, purer.

Shimik danced and cried — a man of seventy-one who had seen enough in his life and didn't know if it would end in sorrow or joy.

Now came time for the sixth *hakafah*. The man wrapped in a tallis approached the *gabbai*, Reb Moshe Gold, and whispered something in his ear. Reb Moshe looked at him in disbelief. Then he lifted his hands and cried, "Reb Shimik Blecher is honored with. . . *Ozer Dalim*."

Shimik felt dizzy. Through the crowd surrounding him he watched as the man wrapped in his tallis removed it from his head.

"You?" cried Shimik when he saw the familiar face. "You, of all people? Have you changed your mind? You thought that my story. . . How did you know?"

"No, I didn't change my mind," said the man. "Your story, though, touched me more than any other I have ever heard in my entire life. At first, I tried to forget it. But I never would have forgiven myself if you would have spent your very last pennies on the *hakafah*. I understand your burning need, and I decided that the time would come when you would know that you had done your share. *Ozer Dalim* is important even without you. For you, it was important to honor it before the members of this shul, and you have dedicated your entire life to that aim. *Nu*. . . I have come here to tell you that *Ozer Dalim* will continue to be precious and important, even if you don't sacrifice your entire life for it."

"Are you certain of that?" Shimik asked the stranger.

"Yes," he said. "With all my heart. As certain as I am that my name is Yussel Shailover."

The Man from 3G

E very Adar, year after year, the tenants of the apartment building on 51 Narkis Street were filled with worry, even though they all knew by heart the saying, "When Adar arrives joy increases."

Veterans in the neighborhood remembered that ten years ago they had been, along with their fellow Jews everywhere, accustomed to feel joy in their hearts with the coming of the month of Adar. This custom had changed with the arrival in their midst of the man on the third floor.

No matter how you looked at this neighbor, he was considered a quiet man. Actually, there was hardly anyone in the neighborhood who could testify to having heard from him a sentence longer than, "Yes, sir," save for the janitor, who was willing to testify that the man had once murmured the sentence, "Pardon me, I didn't notice."

Mr. 3G lived alone. If he had any relatives anywhere, they apparently preferred to forget this kinship. He didn't have any friends, and if he did, they seemed, on principle, to vigorously oppose personal visits. In any case, they were never seen in the area. About this there was an unspoken agreement among all the tenants of 51 Narkis Street that, despite the well-known dictum "acquire a friend," it would have been hard to find anyone willing to spend even one thin dime to acquire the friendship of the man from 3G.

On the other hand, none of the tenants had a thing against him — no, not a single thing. He paid his fees with admirable precision, spoke politely, was very clean, and hardly ever made noise. Hardly ever, we said. That's because on Purim he would deviate greatly from his habits of the rest of the year.

Actually, it's quite probable that the building's residents would not even have been aware of the existence of the man from 3G if not for Purim.

On Purim, he made sure to proclaim his existence in a most unusual manner. Every year he would hold a private cantorial concert in the "auditorium" that during the rest of the year served as his apartment, in front of an audience consisting of one man, who was none other than himself.

Apparently, Mr. 3G considered himself to be a great cantor with an unusually pleasant voice, even though no one else other than he was of the same opinion. To tell the truth, many people in the neighborhood maintained that his chances of being accepted as a cantor in any synagogue on the face of the globe were no greater than those of a raven being accepted for that same position. Of course, not a single one of them dared share even a glimmer of this opinion with the man himself — especially since it was only a hunch, both about their neighbor. . . and about the raven as well.

One way or another, the man from 3G believed with all his heart that he had a beautiful voice and ignored the fact that he was the only one who held that belief. In fact, the number of fans of his singing could be counted on the fingers of one hand of a doll — even if that hand had fallen off, as do most dolls' hands.

Actually, the tenants of 51 Narkis Street weren't interested in the beliefs of their neighbor and didn't care a whit if he believed he was the most talented singer-chazan ever — except that their neighbor from 3G made sure to put this belief into practice once a year, on Purim, of all days.

Each and every year, from the moment everyone had returned from the evening Megillah reading, the man from 3G would burst into song, singing into a microphone into the wee hours of the night. At first, his neighbors had accepted his craze with equanimity and said nothing to him. One day, though, the man from 3G decided that the audience for his once-a-year concert wasn't large enough, and he therefore saw fit to include all the building's residents, even the neighbors across the street, to his free performance.

And so, the week before Purim, a small truck arrived, filled with microphones and huge amplifiers. The latter were installed in every window of Mr. 3G's home, until his apartment looked like a huge broadcasting system of the type used at massive political rallies against one government or another.

Mr. 3G also made sure to take care of the audience inside the apartment as well, meaning himself, and for that purpose planted a microphone in every corner, according to the size of the room and its relative importance.

The neighbors learned of this a few days before Purim, when Mr. 3G made a number of tests to check the speakers.

All we can say is that when he called out "one," it sounded like a deafening explosion and was followed by a screech from a car on the street below because Mrs. Bernstein, who was at that moment crossing the street, was so startled by the strange, frightening sound emanating from the huge amplifying system that had once been a house, that she dropped her two bags of fruits and vegetables. They scattered all over the road and the drivers caught in the resulting traffic jam had the dubious pleasure of listening to the atrocious sounds of "testing, testing, one, two, three. I repeat..."

And then Purim arrived.

The nightmare began at the end of the Megillah reading with a brief victory speech and continued with the awful singing of Mr. 3G, although calling it "singing" was a flight of fancy when it came to that man's singing.

Unlike previous years, this time the neighbors could not stand the noise. Apparently, progress had brought to the world amplifiers capable of broadcasting to airplanes. Otherwise there was no way to explain the noise which emanated from what was supposed to be apartment 3G.

The neighbors plugged their ears while it was still daylight but when Yisrael from the first floor asked his wife, "What time is it?" and she answered him, "Of course," and when Mr. Caspi asked his wife where his glasses were, and she said that they had already called and said they would come tomorrow afternoon, the patience of all the neighbors broke.

A small conference was held in the lobby, and everyone decided to go up to the third floor and stop the concert, come what may.

They began to go up. The sounds of their neighbor's voice, not to mention the musical accompaniment, pounded in their ears. There's one thing you should know, and that is that Mr. 3G accompanied himself on a very up-to-date organ. The only problem was that, to his great sorrow, he had forgotten how to read music, or perhaps had never known, and therefore the ensuing duet of the man and his organ were like two parallel lines which will never meet. Any similarity between the song and the accompanying notes was coincidental and the listener's responsibility and his alone.

Seven men stood in front of the door and knocked. It was quite optimistic on their part to expect anyone to hear their knocking, with the electronic drums squawking at full volume.

They rang the bell. It seemed that the ring only served to spur on the singer, who revealed new, unknown facets of his organ's personality.

Moshe Openheimer could no longer restrain himself. He thrust out his hand and turned the handle. The door opened, and the eyes of the neighbors beheld their neighbor dressed in his holiday best, aflame with enthusiasm and passion for his singing.

The man did not stop the concert. He pushed the button for automatic music and went over with his microphone to his unexpected guests.

Mr. Caspi cleared his throat. "We wanted to —"

"Yes, of course, come in," Mr. 3G screamed through the speaker. "Come on in and let's make merry."

"But I wanted to —" Mr. Caspi tried again.

"That's okay. There are chairs, come in." Mr. 3G pushed them all into the house and began to dance and sing. Every now and then he would take one of the neighbors with him on a wild dance. The entire situation became decidedly unpleasant.

Upon seeing the unexpected audience which had made its way into his home, Mr. 3G began to do imitations. Unlike his singing, his imitations were superb. One of the neighbors began to chuckle, and the rest followed suit. In a few minutes, they were all holding their stomachs and laughing uncontrollably.

The laughter broke down the barriers between them, and their neighbor from 3G resumed his horrible musical concert and simply forced everyone to participate.

Slowly, more neighbors, and their children, relatives and friends, entered the apartment. The apartment turned into the Purim-iest center in town.

Outside, the traffic stopped. People got out of their cars, and looked up towards the terrible noise and dancing emanating from the third floor.

The dancing swept up the throngs outside, and the street was closed off to traffic. The policemen called in to make order stood at the side, not knowing what to do. Above the clamor, the voice of the neighbor from 3G stood out, and it seemed as if it was the off-key singing and music which made the concert especially successful.

It was twelve o'clock at night. The neighbor from 3G stopped playing and singing, shut the numerous speakers in his apartment, and sank down, exhausted, into his armchair. His neighbors sat down opposite him.

"Ahem," Mr. Caspi cleared his throat. "Listen, we wanted to. . . speak with you about the. . . speakers."

"Yes, I know what you want to say," murmured Mr. 3G. "I, too, felt that the music didn't sound the way it should have, and I apologize to you for not having ordered enough speakers.

"Please understand," their neighbor continued, "I simply didn't plan on your coming to hear me, do you understand? I've been singing like this for hours every Purim for the past ten years. To my dismay, I am unable to do so the rest of the year, and, to tell the truth, I actually have no opportunity to do so. I'm an unhappy man, and unhappy people don't sing.

"Once in a while, I find something small which makes me happy. I guard it zealously. I save it for this day. On a regular day, I am overcome by shame, but on Purim," he added, "on Purim I feel that if I don't release some of the happiness pent up inside me, the sadness and the loneliness, which are my lot the rest of the year, will overcome me.

"I promise you that with Hashem's help, I'll order more speakers next year so that you, too, will be able to enjoy it," their neighbor encouraged them. "Please don't hold it against me. I simply had no idea you would come this year. But next year..."

The neighbors bade him farewell, each going up or down to his own apartment silently, engrossed in thought.

"On the other hand," they heard the voice of their neighbor from 3G calling after them, "please allow me to reconsider my promise of additional speakers. I just thought to myself that Purim is Purim but one must still be considerate of the other neighbors. I may just have to refuse your request.

"However," added their neighbor, "you have to admit that even this way it was pretty happy, too. Don't you agree?"

HaKorim

A year after his first son was born to him, Reb Alexander agreed to serve as the *ba'al tefillah* for the *Yamim Nora'im*.

Year after year, the members of the shul had pleaded with him to take upon himself this task. They knew that he came from a long line of famous cantors who had perished in the Holocaust. Those sitting nearest him in shul used to listen to his sweet *tefillah* with their eyes closed, and that, too, was whispered about. They heard beautiful melodies the likes of which they had never heard before. They listened to his sobbing voice, his broken heart, and knew that they had within their midst an exceptional *ba'al tefillah*. Yet, every year, he refused. "How can I lead the prayer service during the recitation of the priestly service on Yom Kippur? How can I prostrate myself during *HaKorim* when Hashem has denied me sons to help me rise?" he used to say.

It seems that in his family, there was a tradition passed down from generation to generation that a son would *daven* beside his father to help him with the *tefillah* and the ancient melodies which had been handed down throughout the ages, and most important of all, to help his father rise to his feet at the end of *HaKorim*.

"When Hashem blesses me with a son, I will gladly lead the services," he would answer all those who asked.

"If not for everything, at least for Rosh Hashanah," they would plead.

Reb Alexander was stubborn. "I've already said what I had to say," he would cut short the conversation. He knew himself well, and he knew that if he would lead the prayers on Rosh Hashanah, he would be forced to do so on Yom Kippur as well, for if he didn't, it would be a disgrace to his family. Only a chazan deemed unworthy of his position would be prevented from serving on Yom Kippur. "Either I lead the prayers or I don't," he used to say.

The members of the congregation outsmarted him and listened to his exquisitely sung prayers on the sly. It was their good fortune that he prayed with his eyes closed and did not see how all of the shul's members listened in to his private supplications. Sometimes, the listeners' good fortune would increase, and Reb Alexander would be transported back to the days when he had accompanied his father, Reb Binyamin, the famous chazan. Then his memories would make him forget that he was in a public place, that there was another chazan besides him... and that he had no sons.

He would make full use of his powerful yet delicate vocal chords and, plucking them to the breaking point, would emit heart-rending sobs which served as preludes for his rousing rendition. The sounds left his mouth as if no other melody on earth existed, taking the hearts of the other worshipers with them on their voyage to the Heavenly Throne.

His fellow congregants would watch his closed eyes, his tears, his trembling lips, and would feel each time anew that a treasure was in their midst — a priceless treasure, intangible yet a treasure nonetheless, that could only be listened to in secret.

Little did Reb Alexander know that there were many who prayed that he be blessed with a son. Although those prayers had about them a trace of self-interest, in the end, when they thought of the man himself and his noble soul, they became completely sincere.

Nor did he know that the stories about the "chazan who doesn't want to lead the services" had taken wings and that many people came to the Or Meir shul during the *Yamim Nora'im* only to participate in that same stolen listening.

One evening, on the third night of Chanukah to be precise, a date which all of the members of the congregation still remember well, Hashem blessed Reb Alexander and his wife — and all those who prayed for him — with a son.

For the next nine months the members of the community waited with heightened expectations for the *Yamim Nora'im*. They didn't dare ask Reb Alexander, for fear they would hear a no from him. They knew quite well that once that word left his mouth, it would be impossible to change his mind.

Didn't we tell you that Reb Alexander was a stubborn man?

That year, he went up to *daven* before the *amud*.

It was Rosh Hashanah, and Reb Alexander simply walked to the front of the shul and began the service.

Reb Alexander's *daven*ing became the talk of everyone in the neighborhood, and even beyond. Needless to say, all the seats in the shul were sold out during the Ten Days.

On Yom Kippur, Reb Alexander went up to lead the services, and once again melodies never before heard there filled the air. They were sweet, somewhat plaintive melodies, turning suddenly joyous. They swept up the entire congregation and moved the women's section to tears until... the moment came, close to the end of the *tefillah*, to recite the priestly service, *HaKorim*.

To their surprise, the congregants saw that Reb Alexander paused and waited. A moment, which seemed like an eternity, passed, and suddenly the wail of an infant was heard. The baby carriage of Shlomo, the nine-month-old only son of Reb Alexander made its way to the Ark, guided by the experienced hands of Yechezkel the *gabbai*.

The carriage advanced towards the Ark and stopped beside Reb Alexander. Then Reb Alexander broke out into the stirring melody of *HaKorim*. The magical, ethereal melody evoked images of the sacred priests of yore and recaptured the aura of the *Beis HaMikdash* and the ecstasy of the entire nation which pervaded it when the *kohen gadol* uttered the Ineffable Name with purity and sanctity. It was a kind of ancient melody as sad as the distance of those days.

"*Hayu korim* — they would kneel," cried Reb Alexander as he knelt and prostrated himself, touching the floor with his forehead and remaining in that position for a long time until certain that the very last worshiper must have already risen.

And what did he do then if not thrust his hand toward the carriage and clasp the little nine month old's hand and lift himself upwards, as if it was little Shlomo who was pulling him up?

The congregants were astounded and amazed by this incredible scene but in unspoken agreement said nothing. They dared not ask Reb Alexander about this mysterious ceremony, lest it prompt an unexpected decision.

This scene repeated itself the following Yom Kippur, when Shlomo was seated in a stroller, and two years later, when the child, his beautiful long hair gathered by a ribbon, stood on his own two feet and did not seem surprised at all by the scene. Shlomo was absolutely certain with all his heart that it was he who had managed to lift his father who had so suddenly fallen.

When Shlomo was four, he sat beside his father on a small stool and hummed along with him from time to time, without going outside to play. When he was seven, a special low table was placed for him. By that time, he knew nearly all of the melodies and knew, of course, how to help his father rise after *HaKorim*, even though he already understood that his father was really getting up by himself.

By the time Shlomo reached bar mitzvah age, the entire congregation knew that he had inherited his father's magnificent voice. Many were even willing to take the risk of asserting that the son's was better than the father's. However, such things were said in a whisper for fear of angering Reb Alexander.

Truth be told, eventually those whispers did reach the ears of Reb Alexander but for some reason they didn't anger him at all. For many years Reb Alexander had often claimed as much to his wife — and they had even argued about it — and now his view was substantiated.

"Now I can die in peace," Reb Alexander would tell his closest friends. "The family chain has not been broken. Shlomo will continue in my footsteps, G-d willing."

The years passed, and Shlomo became a young man. His voice matured and began to resemble that of his father. His arms were strong and muscular, something which many attributed to his annual effort to lift his father from his prostrate position at *HaKorim*, a job he had been doing since he was almost a year old.

And now that he had reached the age of sixteen, it was clear to see that Reb Alexander was not exerting himself at all when he rose from *HaKorim* but was clearly being pulled up by his son, Shlomo.

Never had Reb Alexander discussed this strange custom with his son but an astute boy like Shlomo fully understood that his father had to do it, and that it was a matter of great importance.

The father and his son, a chazan and his assistant, year after year would lift their voices together in prayer, singing aloud, their trills filling the air, their voices breaking and then in the next moment blending together in wondrous harmony, the two voices as one, as if emanating from one throat, one heart.

And then came different days, sad, difficult times. At first, there were just rumors that were easily dismissed with a wave of the hand. But soon enough, more and more people began seeing Shlomo going around with boys who didn't dress like him, who weren't Torah and mitzvah observant, who weren't able to appreciate Reb Alexander's *tefillah*, for they never, ever *davened*.

One day, Reb Alexander arrived in shul, broken in spirit. The rumors had reached him and been confirmed. Reb Alexander summoned his twenty-year-old son, who did not deny his father's accusations. A sharp exchange took place between the two. No one knew what occurred in the room behind the closed door. Only one broken voice was heard, whose meaning no one understood.

The news spread like wildfire: Reb Alexander had banished his son. "You are not my son," he had told him. "I never want to see you again," he declared, and from then on, he had stood true to his word, despite the pleas of his wife and relatives.

At that point, many people attempted to mediate between Reb Alexander and Shlomo. They tried to cool the father's anger and bring the son back to Torah observance but to no avail. The son became even more distant, took off his yarmulke, and began to sing in theaters and give other performances. Reb Alexander refused to hear about his son's successes or his failures — or anything about him. "I no longer have a son," he proclaimed.

Some tried to reprove the father. "One shouldn't reject the son who has fallen," they'd tell him. "You shouldn't push him away."

Reb Alexander would brush them off scornfully. "They don't understand," he'd say. "They don't understand anything."

Selichos night arrived. Reb Alexander approached the Ark, yet he wasn't the same familiar Reb Alexander everyone knew but rather a shadow of his former self. His beard had turned white, his face, pale, his gaze, disoriented — as if someone had destroyed his entire world.

His voice, though, remained as before, except for the thread of sadness woven throughout. His *tefillah* was sadder and consequently more heart-rending than ever before.

During the Ten Days between Rosh Hashanna and Yom Kippur, the leaders of the community did their utmost to persuade Reb Alexander to lead the prayers on Yom Kippur. There was one question, though, which they could not answer: "Who will help me rise during *HaKorim*?"

Fortunately, Reb Alexander did not ask that question. He sat in silence. One could see in him a certain indecision, a sense of doubt.

Yom Kippur arrived, and the congregation waited for *mussaf*, for the recitation of, "Here I am impoverished of deeds...," the prayer with which the chazan begins *mussaf*. All were thoroughly familiar with Reb Alexander's liturgy, and feared that they might never again hear him chant it.

Yet he approached the Ark and prayed as he had never wept before; wept as he had never sung before; sung as he had never trilled before. And one old man, the oldest man there, said, "That's it. That's the voice of Reb Binyamin, the great chazan of Warsaw."

And who was Reb Binyamin, if not the father of Reb Alexander?

The *tefillah* proceeded slowly, until the chazan reached the Order of the Priestly Service. He began to sing, his voice about to break, until he reached the word, "*v'hakohanim.*"

He paused and leaned on the Ark, his eyes shut.

The congregation held its breath.

And then, there was a rustling from the back. Silently, a curly-hair man, obviously only temporarily wearing the yarmulke perched on top of his head, neared the Ark.

Shlomo.

He stood next to his father, who didn't even acknowledge his presence with a nod. Reb Alexander began to sing "*HaKorim,*" and suddenly, as in days gone by, the voice of his son was heard accompanying him.

"When they heard the glorious, awesome, Ineffable Name," Reb Alexander sang out, "emanate from the mouth of the High Priest" — and here their voices harmonized as always, Reb Alexander's the lower one and Shlomo's the higher — "in holiness and purity.

"*Hayu korim.*"

The entire congregation knelt and hastened to rise in order to view the most terrible sight of all.

Shlomo held on to his father in order to lift him, but when Reb Alexander stood, he pushed Shlomo away, saying, "You're not my son," and continued the melody.

Everyone cried. Wailing was heard from the women's section. Shlomo looked embarrassed and hurt. He turned from his place and walked towards the doorway.

Only Reb Alexander continued to pray.

The following year, the scene repeated itself. Shlomo came to shul in time for the Order of the Priestly Service, accompanied his father's melodies, knelt with him, raised him, was thrust aside, and left.

Everyone cried and could not forget those short moments until that rejection. The broken voices of the father and son, their hearts one, yet shattered.

Over the years, Shlomo became a famous performer. Everyone knew he was the son of Torah-observant parents and had gone astray. He did not deny it, and even agreed to talk about it, and in the same breath, blasphemed all that is sacred with his every word.

But when he was asked about his parents, he preferred to move on to the next question.

Year after year, the same scene repeated itself. In time, Shlomo married and began to bring his small son to shul with him, at first in a carriage and, later on, on his own two feet. The child grew. He never spoke with his grandfather, and it was evident that it was hard for him to understand what was going on, since that world was completely foreign to him.

Shlomo's friends learned about his custom of attending shul on Yom Kippur and regarded it as an amusing pastime. One time they decided to come to shul to see for themselves. Seeing the father rejecting his son before the entire congregation, and hearing the cries of the men, the weeping of the women, they understood that the scene was no ordinary one. They left in shock.

"Why do you stand for such humiliation?" they asked Shlomo after he left the shul. "What do you get from that man who only disgraces you?"

Shlomo answered, "I have my dividends."

They didn't understand him. But then again, why should they?

Of course, Shlomo arrived in shul the following Yom Kippur, too.

He was thirty-eight by then, while his father was approaching seventy-two. For eighteen years they hadn't spoken to each other, except for that same strange meeting each year when the father would thrust his son aside. Once more, Shlomo appeared in shul on time for the Priestly Order of Service. Once more, he planned to help his father rise.

That year had been a difficult one for Reb Alexander and his wife. Not only had old age taken its toll but Reb Alexander had been burdened by emotional turmoil as well. He would sit on his porch from morning until night, staring at a mysterious point. Sometimes, he would cringe, as if he had seen a nightmare. And sometimes, Reb Alexander would weep, something he hadn't done since childhood, except for those hours when he raised his voice in prayer. He would sit on the porch and weep.

Then a new era dawned, during which Reb Alexander neither wondered nor wept, neither spoke nor hardly ate. All he did was sit on the porch, his face clouded with sadness.

His wife would tread through the house silently, afraid to disturb him. But about what, then, could she speak to him? About their rebellious, wanton son? About his contemptuous words of scorn for all things holy, which had drawn the laughs of a crowd just this very week?

Those days were full of suffering. If only Reb Alexander had said the word, his son would have come to visit him, to talk with him. But Reb Alexander said nothing.

And then Yom Kippur arrived.

As usual, Reb Alexander approached the Ark, and even before he opened his mouth a pall of sadness descended upon the congregation. All knew of the suffering of this sorrowful, elderly man and wondered what pushed him to come and make his voice, still sweet and with the same thread of sadness, heard.

That Yom Kippur, Shlomo once again came at the designated time, and again the voices of father and son blended as they did every year, along with the emotional, somewhat frightening scene.

When they reached *HaKorim*, Reb Alexander remained prostrate much longer than usual, and Shlomo, who sensed that something was amiss, raised him and saw something in his face that he hadn't seen in the past eighteen years. They stood heart to heart, and suddenly Shlomo cried out, "Bring a doctor!" and placed his father on the floor.

For the first time, Shlomo wept. There, sitting on the floor next to his father, whom they were attempting to revive, he needed no doctor to tell him that his father was no longer among the living.

There was no doubt about it — for his father had not pushed him away.

On Sukkos, after the shortened shiva week, Shlomo appeared in shul to recite Kaddish.

He continued to do so throughout the rest of the year, and journalists began to publish reports about the "repentant return" of the "famous performer."

Shlomo did not deny the rumors, yet neither did he confirm them. One day, a number of his good friends — artists, actors, and journalists — came to try to "shake him up," as they say. Throughout the entire meeting Shlomo remained silent, even though silence wasn't characteristic of him. When his friends finished speaking, he agreed to say only this: "You don't understand. You don't understand a thing. Didn't you see that my father needed me?"

"Is that why he used to push you away and humiliate you every year?" one of them asked.

"Perhaps you don't know," Shlomo told them, "that every year, a moment before that same humiliating push, my father would hold on to me for a brief instant. No one else saw this. Only the two of us knew about it. Only he and I knew clearly at that same instant that if I wouldn't have held him, he would have fallen to the floor.

"My father held on to me, do you understand?" wept Shlomo. "My father signaled to me that he still needed me. True, he was still angry at me and had even despaired of me but he still needed me! I knew that he needed me to perpetuate the family chain.

"Yes, every year, during that brief moment, my father would convey everything he had refrained from saying all year. Did you think I would refuse to help my father?"

On the following Yom Kippur, lifting his melodious voice in prayer before the Ark stood the congregation's new *ba'al tefillah*, Reb Shlomo. Next to him stood his son, singing with him. He knew all the melodies, for he had stood beside his father and grandfather all those years.

His father had never explained the family custom but a clever lad like he fully understood that he had to stand next to his father so that he could help him rise from *HaKorim*.

And when the two stood heart to heart, the strong youth holding his weeping father, who had just risen from *HaKorim*, the two singing the ancient melodies in perfect harmony, the congregation burst into tears, just as it had during all those years, as if nothing had changed.

All who witnessed that scene sensed the spirit of unity between the father and his son, and were at long last able to smile and say, "Hashem has returned the hearts of the fathers to their sons, and the hearts of the sons to their fathers."

A Plain, Ordinary Woman

"I'm just a plain, ordinary woman," she told Mrs. Cohen, the school principal who looked at her with penetrating eyes. "I know how to type a bit and write letters. With Hashem's help, I'll be a good secretary for the school."

The principal didn't answer. The lull in the conversation created a stifling silence, and Nira felt forced to fill the gap. "I'm really interested in the position. I'll be very responsible."

Silence. The principal glanced at Nira's résumé: "Meital, Nira, *ba'alas teshuvah*, married for two years to a *ba'al teshuvah* who learns in a yeshivah. Previous place of work: the Shefa factory."

"What did you do at Shefa?" the principal asked.

"I worked in the marketing department."

Mrs. Cohen found it difficult to imagine Nira loading trucks. Perhaps she had been a cleaning lady?

"Do you know how to use a computer? I'm sure you've noticed that we have one in our office."

"Yes, you could say so. I think I'll be able to manage."

The principal sighed deeply. The rabbi who had recommended Nira had said that she was intelligent. Had he perhaps exaggerated a bit? As if reading Mrs. Cohen's mind, Nira said, "I'll do whatever you ask of me. It's fine. I'm a plain, ordinary woman."

The principal was almost ready to reject her but changed her mind at the last minute. "Fine. Please come in tomorrow morning, and we'll see how things work out."

Nira shook Mrs. Cohen's hand warmly, thanked her and turned to leave.

"Nira," the principal called after her in a worried tone which betrayed her misgivings.

"Yes?"

"I hope you'll manage with the computer."

"I'll try," replied Nira. "Thank you."

After Nira left, Mrs. Cohen stared out the window, wondering whether her decision to hire Nira was good for the school or not.

"A plain, ordinary woman," she repeated out loud. "That's well and good — but it depends for what."

The following morning, Nira arrived promptly, sat down at her desk, and waited for her first assignment.

She was soon busy typing letters on an old type-writer, pasting stamps on envelopes, answering the phone and taking messages. Two hours later, one of the teachers walked into the office and asked Nira to create a worksheet for her English class. It was a grammar drill and involved filling in the missing words in a word-usage chart. The lay-out was complex.

When the principal overheard the teacher's request, she realized that she really should go over and help the new secretary so that she wouldn't be embarrassed by her lack of proficiency.

"Are you familiar with word processing?" the principal asked Nira.

"Word processing? I guess so," Nira answered quietly.

"Here," said the principal as she leaned over the keyboard. "This is Enter, and this is Backspace. Now type something. Good," she said encouragingly. "Do you think you can handle it?"

"I guess so."

"It's not easy to set up a chart, and this one is a bit difficult for a beginner, so I'll do that part for you and you can just fill in the words."

"Fine."

The principal set up the chart on the screen and watched to see how Nira would manage with entering the words.

"Very good," the principal complimented her. "I see that you catch on easily."

Was that a glimmer of a smile she noticed on Nira's face?

That day, the principal returned home satisfied. "I didn't make a mistake," she told herself. "She's catching on nicely. I think she'll work out just fine."

The days flowed by like the rivers of material Nira processed. Sometimes the principal would, on her own, come over to help her.

"You can speed things up by doing a search and replace. Here, all you have to do is go to Edit and then Replace..."

Nira nodded. Watched patiently and nodded. Sometimes, though, when Mrs. Cohen would ask a question in the slightest way personal, Nira would murmur, "Oh, I'm just a plain, ordinary woman."

Months later, when the school year was about to end, Mrs. Cohen felt that Nira had more than proven her sincerity and devotion. She was never absent, never late, and sometimes even took work home. "True, I still don't trust her with the more complex computer work — I do that myself — but there's no doubt about it, I made the right decision."

Soon it was time for the annual school trip. Grades 1 through 3 were invited to the Shefa factory. The secretary had arranged the trip. After all, she had once worked there.

The day before the trip, when one of the teachers called to say she would be unable to participate, the principal asked Nira to take her place.

That was the first time since she had begun working there that Nira had ever tried to refuse a request. The principal was surprised. "Please come, Nira," she urged. "If you come, so will I."

Nira shrugged her shoulders. "Okay, so be it. But do me a favor — you take charge. I don't think I can manage... I'm just a plain, ordinary woman."

The principal, who already knew that, nodded. "Don't worry. Everything will be fine."

The buses reached the gates of the huge factory. The girls got off and walked toward the entrance where one of the company's employees awaited them, her eyes searching the crowd. Suddenly she spotted Nira.

"Nira!" she called out. "How are you?"

"Fine," Nira replied with obvious discomfort. Soon, though, the two were deep in conversation as they walked inside. There stood a man impeccably dressed in a suit and tie — the manager. "Give this school the special tour," he directed his staff. "It's a pity you left us," he said, turning to

Nira, "and to become a school secretary, no less! I simply can't understand it. . ."

Mrs. Cohen, the principal, who had heard every word, also didn't understand. Wasn't it a step up to go from being a factory worker to a school secretary? What didn't he understand? What lowering of status had there been here?

Mrs. Cohen's surprise intensified when she heard Nira reply with unusual confidence, "You'd be surprised how much of a step up it is in my eyes."

The manager gave her a look of deep pity. "Well, let's not argue about levels but what about salary? Here you made ten times what you're making there, right?"

Nira nodded vigorously. "I have different priorities nowadays than money. That incentive no longer interests me. My husband also left his job. Now he studies in a yeshivah."

"Yossi? Left Elbit? What happened to him? What happened to both of you? You were at the top — why did you jump off?"

"We wanted to stand on firm ground," she replied with a smile. "We were tired of floating and aspiring to the heights and attaining them while still being on such a low level. Nowadays we aspire to other heights. Practical ones. Today we are simple, ordinary people in every way."

While they talked, the three of them, Mrs. Cohen, Nira and the manager, had walked toward the marketing department. They now entered a luxurious room whose walls were lined with huge computer screens the likes of which the principal had never before seen in her life. Around the room, people were bent over their keyboards.

"Nira!" A voice broke the silence. Heads looked up in surprise, and soon everyone had left his computer to hurry over to the door.

Some approached her with large printouts, asking her questions about the data and consulting with her on how to proceed. One person called her over to a screen to show her the projected sales distribution of a certain product, charted according to region.

The principal looked at her secretary and suddenly discovered in her an extraordinary amount of self-confidence and authority. She watched the other workers and saw in their faces the respect and deference they felt for this "plain, ordinary woman" who had worked for her for the past year.

The realization that she had never really known her secretary dawned on her. Turning to one of the clerks, she pointed to Nira and asked, "Who is she?"

"Don't you know? That's Nira, the former director of Shefa's computerized marketing department. She's one of the best programmers in the country!"

The principal stepped outside and walked over to the window. The glass reflected her stunned expression. Suddenly she felt an arm around her shoulder. She turned and saw Nira standing next to her.

Silence.

At last, the principal regained her composure. Turning to Nira, she apologized. "I'm sorry I didn't appreciate you enough. I thought you were just a plain, ordinary woman."

"But that's exactly what I want to be!" Nira replied. "A plain, ordinary woman."

The Saga
of the
Afikomen

It was the most ordinary of Seder nights. Around the wide, massive table sat the entire Jakobowitz family. They were the sons and daughters of ninety-year-old Reb Yechezkel Jakobowitz, his sons-in-law, daughters-in-law, his married grandchildren and their families, a few elderly people who had been invited, just like every year, from the nearby nursing home, and several dozen great-grandchildren, some of whom sat and some of whom ran around, between, and over the chairs.

They all knew that this year, just as every year, a very special Seder awaited them — a Seder which would last into the wee hours of the night, one at which Grandpa Yechezkel would open his usually locked tongue and heart and retell in his unique way the story of the Exodus from Egypt. One detail, though, marred the rejoicing and anticipation. Not only this year but every year.

The *afikomen*.

Never ever had anyone managed to continue the custom of taking the *afikomen* in Grandpa Yechezkel's house. Grandpa Yechezkel would guard it zealously, as if it were diamonds glued to the crown of the King of England — and chances were that that king guarded those expensive pieces of glass a lot less carefully than the way Grandpa Yechezkel guarded the *afikomen*.

Throughout the years, his children, grand-children, and great-grandchildren had grown accustomed to Grandpa Yechezkel's strange stubbornness and no longer troubled him about the *afikomen*.

The only guests at the Seder who complained each and every year about this custom of Grandpa Yechezkel's were the elderly men and women from the nearby nursing home. Every year, Grandpa Yechezkel would invite two or three of the old people to join him for the Seder. They were bitter and ailing people, who had one thing in common: None of them could reconcile himself to the fact that Grandpa Yechezkel did not permit his great-grandchildren to take the *afikomen*.

Thus, dozens of years and Seders passed for Grandpa Yechezkel without him ever losing a single *afikomen*.

❧ Chapter Two

In the year in which our story takes place, the entire Jakobowitz family gathered as usual, with the addition of two elderly people whom Grandpa Yechezkel had, as usual, taken in from the nearby old-age home.

The Seder commenced with Grandpa Yechezkel's explicit warning against taking the *afikomen* hidden under his coat. As usual, the warning prompted an outburst of whispers, and even some outright criticism, from the elderly guests who had been invited that year.

After eating the bitter herbs, Grandpa Yechezkel took out the matzah, wrapped the larger piece in his huge handkerchief, and hid it under his coat.

Silence prevailed, and Grandpa Yechezkel began to tell the story of the Exodus. Closing his eyes, he was transported back to those distant days when he had left Egypt along with the other Jews. He told about the differences of opinion between Dasan and Aviram, and Moshe, the leader. He told those sitting around the table thirsting for his words about the moment he had stood facing the raging sea and how he had hesitated to jump. All listened in silence.

Suddenly, Grandpa Yechezkel paused.

He shifted in his seat. Everyone looked at him with concern, waiting for him to continue his gripping tale.

"Where is the *afikomen*?" he asked.

"The *afikomen*?"

"Someone took the *afikomen*, and I demand that he return it to me immediately," he ordered.

No one budged.

"I appeal to whoever took the *afikomen* to return it," he repeated in a stern, cold voice.

Silence.

Again and again Grandpa Yechezkel stated his request, but to no avail.

The sons turned to the grandchildren, and they to the great-grandchildren. The one who took it was not discovered. Searches were made but the *afikomen* was not found.

"I see I have no choice," said Grandpa Yechezkel, "but to tell you why I don't let anyone take the *afikomen* from me. I am certain it will convince the person who took it to return it to me."

Shock. None of those present had ever over all those years dreamed that there was a story behind Grandpa

Yechezkel's entrenched stubbornness. All listened raptly as he began to speak.

❧ *Chapter Three*

"Among the residents of the small Ukrainian town in which I lived," began Grandpa Yechezkel, "was a young boy named Mordechai, whom everyone called 'Mottel the Thief.' This same Mordechai owned a pair of hands that were unusually clever. The rumor amongst the town's children was that Mottel the Thief was able to lock a drawer so fast that he could manage to sneak the key back into it, too.

"He used to demonstrate this agility to everyone. The children would gather around him, and he would show them tricks like pulling objects out of their pockets without their even noticing it. The small fee Mottel the Thief would charge for his demonstration was usually a bit of food to allay his pangs of hunger.

"One day, one of the *melamdim* lost his gold watch. The entire *cheder* searched for the valuable lost item, and a thorough investigation was conducted throughout the town. At the end of the investigation, the watch was found in the home of an aunt of Mottel, who had, for some reason, been absent from *cheder* that day. Mottel claimed that he had found the watch on one of the streets and added that he had planned to announce his find. But in light of his reputation, there were those who assumed that he had seasoned his theft with lies, and therefore, after heavy pressure, which they troubled themselves to apply to the *cheder*'s principal, he was thrown out of the *cheder* forever.

"From that day on, Mottel began to roam the streets like a vagabond. At first, he mingled with the peddlers in the marketplace, completely at home, until a theft was discovered there, too, and they hastened to chase him away — but not before giving him a sound thrashing in the hopes that it would shake out a few of the gold coins he had stolen. From then on, he wandered from place to place but wherever he went, there were those who decided, without investigating matters thoroughly, that Mottel the Thief was a first-class troublemaker of the worst kind, and perhaps even worse than that.

"And so, Mottel the Thief was considered what we now call a juvenile delinquent. The stories rumored about his behavior were hair-raising. Several times he had even been arrested by the police and had spent time in jail. Thus spread the bad name they had given Mottel, until many parents, convinced of his guilt, refused to allow their children to associate with him, and not only out of doubt."

↜ Chapter Four

Grandpa Yechezkel paused in his story. Everyone listened intently, save for the two oldsters who dozed, mistaking their reclining cushions for pillows.

"And then" — Grandpa Yechezkel took up his story again — "the year 1914 arrived, and World War I broke out, bringing chaos to the Ukraine. Poles, Bolsheviks, White Russians and Ukrainian nationalists made pogroms on the Jews. They were days of fear and terror. No one knew what the morrow would bring.

"In our large town in the southern part of the Ukraine, a man named Nester Ivanowitz Mechno, may his name be blotted out, began to cast his reign of terror. Mechno had been sentenced to life imprisonment in 1908 but was released from prison with the outbreak of the revolution and began to fight against the White Russians, the opponents of the Bolsheviks. He gained control of the northern Ukraine after vanquishing all his enemies. Wherever he took over, he gave orders to annihilate those he hated most — the Jews.

"One hundred thousand Jews were massacred in those pogroms," cried Grandpa Yechezkel. "Do you hear? One hundred thousand Jews. I knew many of them. The rabbi of our community, Reb Shmaya, the *melamed*, Reb Leibele, and at least five of my classmates: Reuve'le, Yossel, Shmelke, Yisruel, and my very best friend, Yekusiel Reizman."

Grandpa Yechezkel's voice broke. A mournful mood pervaded the room.

"And then Seder night arrived. The entire family sat around the table. From afar, gunshots and the screams of rioters were heard. We hoped they wouldn't reach us. My father, may he rest in peace, told the story of the Exodus just as he did every year — in the very same manner I am telling it to you today. I crept under the table and crawled towards him to take the *afikomen*. Silently, I made it to his legs. I thrust my hand behind the pillow where he sat and took the *afikomen*. I felt that my father moved a little from his place so that I would be able to do it but I was never ever able to ask him about it.

"I began to creep back to my place and then... a tremendous noise was heard! The door burst open and everyone in the house began to scream in terror.

"I heard several shots, shouts and screams. I heard my father shout, '*Ahergt nisht di maidel* — Don't kill the girl.' A few more shots were fired. A body fell to the floor. I heard a broken cry. I saw many feet around the table. I recognized the nailed boots of the rioters. I remained huddled where I was, hoping they wouldn't lift the large tablecloth. The tumult and killing continued.

"From under the table I saw how they dragged my father along the floor. He managed to whisper to me, '*Chatzkel, zi a yid; fargestnigt du darfst mir tzurikgeben der afikoimen* — Yechezkel, remain a Jew; and don't forget that you have to return the *afikomen* to me.' After that, the noise died down and a terrifying silence prevailed.

"I remained huddled under the table, trembling. I didn't dare move from my place. I didn't even cry. Fear had totally immobilized me.

"I sat that way the entire night. Seder night in 1917.

"When I finally had the courage to get out, I discovered that the mob had taken my entire family with them, except for my small sister, Raizele, and my grandmother Sheindel, whose bodies I found under the table.

"I sat beside the cold bodies and wept until the source of my tears ran dry. I didn't know what to do. Suddenly I saw that I was still clutching the large handkerchief with the *afikomen*. It seems that while I had sat frightened and trembling under the table, I had unknowingly crushed the matzah into tiny pieces. I remembered well my father's final request and decided to search for him and return the *afikomen* to him."

❧ Chapter Five

"I went outside. The houses were destroyed and not a soul was seen. I walked about aimlessly until I met a fellow townsman. It was none other than Mottel the Thief. At first I tried to hide and run but he grabbed my arm and asked me what I was doing. I told him that I was going to look for my father. He laughed strangely and told me that to do that I'd have to go up to Heaven. I didn't understand what he meant.

"I told him I thought it was more dangerous to go with him than without him. He made a sour face and disappeared. I continued on. I felt very hungry. Before I could think of what to do, I found myself face to face with someone who looked like one of Mechno's men, may his name be blotted out.

"He drew closer to me with a menacing gait. I remained rooted to my place. He raised the ax which he was carrying. Suddenly, a cry was heard: 'Leave him alone, he's mine.'

"It was Mottel again. The man saw him and left. I saw Mottel was dressed in the uniform of one of Mechno's men, the same ones who had killed my family. 'Go away,' I shouted at him. 'Look who you're helping!'

" 'Fool,' he hissed at me. 'Do you think I joined Mechno's men? I "borrowed" this uniform from one of his officers, who is apparently still bathing in the river at this very moment.'

"I froze," said Grandpa Yechezkel, "and afterwards I said, 'I almost forgot that there are those who call you Mottel the Thief. I hope you steal only from murderers and not from Jews.'

"Mottel's face darkened, and I thought he was about to finish the work of the owner of the ax but instead he merely replied, 'Would you like to join me?'

"I thought a bit and decided that in this difficult time, with my life in danger, I couldn't be choosy about my friends. I knew I had to return the *afikomen* to my father, and that to do so, I needed Mottel's help.

"We left the city and headed toward the forest. At first, Mottel took advantage of his quick hands and stealth to take food out of the homes of the murderers. However, the further we got from town, the harder it became for Mottel to get food — that's because there weren't any more people to steal from. Soon we were overcome by real pangs of hunger.

"At a certain point, when both of us were extremely hungry and tried to pick a few wild plants to eat, the thought crossed my mind that most likely Mottel might want to search my pockets for the *afikomen* I had to return to my father. I quickly removed it from my pocket and tried to hide it in one of my socks. However, it was quite naive of me to think that such an attempt could escape the eagle-eyed gaze of Mottel the Thief. He threw himself at me, saying, 'What are you hiding there?'

" 'The *afikomen*!'

"I tried to convince him that it was the *afikomen* that I took from my father and which I had to return to him but Mottel was certain that I was trying to trick him and eat it myself without sharing my meal with him. Mottel the Thief was furious. He felt that I was unbelievably ungrateful. When he reminded me of all the food he had given me, I told him, 'But this food isn't mine,' and he said, 'If you stole the matzah you're holding, I'm allowed to steal it from you because it says, "One who steals from a thief is not guilty." '

"At this point, a scholarly argument began between us which drew me to the conclusion that this Mottel must have looked into a Gemara now and then — and according to what he knew, it seemed to me he had looked into a lot of Gemaras.

"At the end of the argument, Mottel informed me that 'even if you'd guard the food in your possession from the very beginning of the watch, I, Mottel, the son of Yeedle, would be able to take it from you — even if you'd hide it under your very skin. But,' he continued, 'I am an honest person and not a thief, and if you insist on guarding the matzah, I'll let you. But woe to you if you eat it without me!'

"Naturally I thought Mottel the Thief's warning was funny, because I had never seen a professional deny his occupation with such conviction as had Mottel the Thief denied being a thief. At that moment I was certain that a law should be passed prohibiting such denials. However, because there was no one in the forest who would approve my proposal, I decided to treat Mottel the Thief with the utmost caution and vigilance, and guard the *afikomen* which belonged to my father as carefully as possible, so that it would not fall into his hands."

❧ Chapter Six

"One day, we found ourselves face to face with a group of Ukrainian nationalists who swarmed in the forests. They opened fire on us, and before I was able to run a few steps, I felt a sharp pain in my leg. I ran another few steps, stumbled, and fell into a ditch on the side of the road. Mottel disappeared.

"The murderers began to search for me. I heard their footsteps and curses clearly, and suddenly I felt that I was on the verge of death. Nothing mattered to me. The sharp pain I felt engulfed me entirely. I regretted only one thing — that I wouldn't be able to return the *afikomen* to my father.

"Suddenly, I saw Mottel crawling towards me. I knew right away that he wanted to take the *afikomen* away from me. I put it under my shirt and greeted him with a hail of kicks. Mottel looked surprised. He grabbed both my hands. I tried to resist but then I fainted from the pain in my legs.

"I awoke in a dark, narrow hut. I felt that someone was with me, taking care of my legs. Straining my eyes to see in the dimness, I saw Mottel wrapping a piece of cloth around my bleeding leg.

"Immediately I stuck my hand under my shirt and was amazed to discover that the *afikomen* was still there.

" 'If you're still worried about the *afikomen*, it's a sign you're okay,' I heard Mottel's voice.

" 'But why?'

" 'Why what?'

" 'Why didn't you take the *afikomen*? Isn't that what you wanted to do?'

" 'Chatzkel, I may be called a thief but I'm not a murderer!' "

❧ Chapter Seven

"Mottel continued to care for me until I recovered. Somehow, we learned that there had been a change in the legal status of the Jews because of some revolt called the 'Communist Revolution,' which had taken place in 1917. We decided to make our way home.

"The way back was fraught with miracles. Many tried to kill us. But our hardest battle was the one fought against our constant enemy, hunger.

"Mottel kept his promise and never tried to take the *afikomen* away from me, even though he repeatedly told me that in such a life-threatening situation, '*pikuach nefesh* overrides the mitzvah of *afikomen*,' an expression he must have coined himself, since it does not appear anyplace.

"When we neared our hometown, we learned that the change in the legal status of the Jews had not reached Mechno's men, or, if it had, they opposed it on principle. Before we could say the word 'revolution,' we found ourselves in a huge camp run by Mechno's henchmen for the thousands of Jews they intended to wipe out.

"As soon as we arrived, we encountered Jews from our town who knew Mottel and were familiar not only with his quick hands but with the derogatory nickname that had been stuck on to him, Mottel the Thief. Mottel's profession was now considered very prestigious, in light of the terrible starvation prevalent in the camp. Mottel went into action, and from that day on, food items began to disappear from the storerooms of the murderers.

"The missing food reached us via Mottel, who distributed his booty to everyone who asked. And there were many who asked. What was strange was that none of the camp's inmates bothered to thank Mottel for the food which saved their lives, and, in fact, all continued to regard him as a lowly thief. Even more than that, when they came to him and asked him for food, they used the name 'Mottel the Thief.' Mottel was hurt but continued to provide them with the supplies they asked for, which, while not costing him his life, came at the price of his endangering it."

Grandpa Yechezkel looked at his listeners to see if they were paying attention, took a deep breath, and continued his story.

"Soon enough, the matter of the disappearing supplies became known to the camp's authorities, and one day a high-ranking officer appeared and ordered all of the camp's inmates to assemble in the central square.

"We waited, and suddenly Mottel appeared, dragged by two young soldiers. We could see he had been beaten from head to toe.

" 'We have received information that this man has taken food from our storerooms,' declared the officer. 'All of you remained silent. Therefore, the thief, along with another hundred Jews, will be taken out and killed.'

"A wave of fear swept over the crowd. Only Mottel remained calm.

"The officer faced Mottel, aimed his gun at him, and said, 'Do you have anything to say before you die?'

" 'Yes,' said Mottel. 'I am not a thief. I am an honest man. True, I take food from your storerooms but that is because you — you murderers! — want to destroy the Jews imprisoned here. I have fulfilled the mitzvah of saving lives,' declared Mottel, and added, 'I am proud that you are planning to kill me because I stole from murderers for Jews. That's all.'

" '*Plan* to kill you?' laughed the officer. 'We are going to kill you right now!'

" 'Plan to,' repeated Mottel with emphasis. 'You won't succeed!'

"The officer lifted his gun and aimed straight for Mottel's heart. We all held our breaths.

He squeezed the trigger. A hollow click was heard.

He squeezed again and again and again. Nothing but clicks.

" 'Who stole the ammunition clip?' shouted the officer.

"Mottel looked at him and calmly answered, 'Me.' Suddenly, with amazing speed, he took the clip out of his pocket, struck the officer in his face with it, grabbed his gun, and with a practiced hand inserted the clip, shot him and his two comrades and shouted, 'Jews, to the gate!' "

❧ Chapter Eight

"It was a massive escape. Mottel fired a bullet at the gate's lock, and thousands of Jews ran outside. The Ukrainians did not stand idly by but began shooting in all directions. Many fell wounded or dead but the vast majority escaped. As I ran, I kept my eyes on Mottel, who was also running and who would, every so often, turn around and with amazing precision, fire at the shooting Ukrainians. Suddenly, he fell.

"I made it over to him. 'Mottel! What happened?' I asked.

" 'Nothing,' he said. 'Keep running.'

"I turned him over. Blood was gushing from a small hole in his chest.

" 'Mottel, you're wounded,' I said. 'Wait and I'll bandage you.'

" 'Run,' Mottel whispered to me. 'I'm finished.'

"It took all my strength to pick him up. I started dragging him to one of the destroyed, abandoned buildings.

Bullets whistled over our heads, the ground was strewn with bodies but I continued dragging him. He tried to resist, whispering, 'Leave me, Chatzkel. You have to return the *afikomen*, don't you?'

"Suddenly, he fell silent.

"I brought him into a building and laid him down on the floor. I stopped the flow of blood which was pouring from his chest. Suddenly, I felt tears streaming down my face. 'Hold on, Mottel, hold on. . . ,' I whispered to him. 'You must live. You're a good man.'

"Mottel did not answer. 'Now, Mottel?' I cried out to him. 'Now, after we've been through so much? You're brave, Mottel, hang on!'

"I touched him, moved him, stroked his cheek. 'Mottel, get up. We must continue our journey. I can't go on without you.'

"All of a sudden, Mottel opened his eyes. 'Listen, in a few minutes I won't be here anymore. . . These are my last words. I want you to know that I never. . . never stole a single thing from a Jew. . . The name Mottel the Thief is a bad name they stuck me with in my youth. . . only because of my clever hands. I never stole the *melamed*'s watch. I really found it. . . but there was no one to believe me. . . A few people judged me unfavorably and managed to influence others, too. There were a few. . . who. . . believed. . . and in their merit. . . I remained alive and did not die from hunger. . . They were good people. . . They gave me a reason to. . . live and to believe in the world which was so unkind to me. . . '

"Mottel winced in pain, and then continued to speak. 'Nearly everyone called me Mottel the Thief. . . My whole life I went around with the sign of Cain on my forehead. What had I done to deserve it? At first I fought. . . but soon enough. . . I found out that I didn't. . . have a chance. Why did they do this to me?

" 'You too...Chatzkel...You didn't believe me either. You guarded your *afikomen* because you were sure I
would steal it...Believe me...I could have...But I'm not a
thief. Your suspicions hurt so much...'

" 'Mottel,' I answered him. 'Forgive me. Maybe it's
too late but in time I did learn to appreciate you. I believe
you, really and truly. You are not a thief, Mottel. You are a
good and honest man. I will clear your name, I promise.'

"Mottel struggled against his pains. 'Hold on,' I cried
out to him with tear-filled eyes. 'I'm willing to die for you...'

"A somewhat frightening smile crossed his lips. 'Do
you know...I never thought anyone would be pained by my
death...It's a shame that I had to die to see it...

" 'Go in peace, Chatzkel,' said Mottel in a barely
audible voice. 'Remember that Mottel is not a thief...only
much maligned. Do you believe me?'

" 'I believe you,' I promised.

"And Mottel closed his eyes.

"Chatzkel sat and cried over Mottel's death. He sat
and lamented the death of a good man who was persecuted
by so many. He contemplated the dead man and the sadness
reflected in his face and wept for a world whose inhabitants
could have so abused one another.

"He looked at the tortured face, for he knew so well
the emotional torment undergone by the pure soul who had
been unjustly suspected."

Grandpa Yechezkel looked at his many offspring,
who were struggling to keep back their tears, and at those
who had lost the battle, and concluded his story:

"Afterwards I covered Mottel's face with a piece of
cloth and, under a hail of bullets, crawled away from the
area, broken in heart and spirit. Nothing mattered to me
anymore. Only hours later, when I was in the middle of the
forest, did I reach for my pocket and discover that it, and the

afikomen, had apparently been completely torn off during our mad flight from the camp. I knew then that I would never be able to return the *afikomen* to my father — not in this world and not in the World to Come. Mottel was dead, the *afikomen* was lost, and I was left with nothing!

"Now do you understand why I so adamantly refuse to let anyone steal my *afikomen*?" Grandpa Yechezkel ended his tale.

✨ The End

The Seder table suddenly looked sad. The guests did not move. They were wrapped in deep thought. True sorrow was seen on their faces over the fate of Mottel, who had suddenly entered their hearts and their lives. The two elderly guests seemed to have been aroused from their slumber as a result of the sudden pause in Grandpa Yechezkel's monologue, which had filled the room for an hour.

Suddenly, the voice of one of the elderly guests, who had awakened from his nap, was heard. "Do you know something? I come from the same region, and it seems to me that you're not quite accurate in some of the details."

Silence fell. Grandpa Yechezkel turned an enraged face to the old man. "Which details, pray tell?"

"First of all, Mottel the Thief did not die, not even once. I know that he lived for many years afterwards. He only lost consciousness, and when he regained it, what do you think he found between the folds of his blanket, if not your *afikomen*?"

Shocked silence. Grandpa Yechezkel turned pale. He said nothing. The old man continued. "According to what I heard, he found you in the end and even returned the *afikomen* to you."

"That's a lie!" cried Grandpa Yechezkel. "I have never seen Mottel since then, and I surely never received the *afikomen* from him. Why are you making fun of an old man who never did you any harm?"

"If you would only conduct a thorough search, you would discover that the *afikomen* is indeed in your possession!"

Instinctively, Grandpa Yechezkel placed his hand inside his coat, and what did he find there, if not two bags, one containing the *afikomen* which had been taken from him about an hour ago, and a second which...

The second bag was none other than a very old handkerchief and...the *afikomen* which he had lost so many years ago! Speechless, Grandpa Yechezkel stared at his elderly guest, unable to say a word.

"Yes," announced the guest, "now I see that a lot of time has passed since the time you zealously guarded the *afikomen* from Mottel the Thief. You've grown old, Chatzkel, and the proof is that you didn't even notice how I took one *afikomen* from inside your coat, and even less than that, how I replaced it with two. The only question left is, did so much time pass that you don't remember your undesired companion? Look at me — don't recognize Mottel the Thief?"

Such Enemies!

One sunless day, the shul's *gabbai*, Yitzchak Trunk, made one of the gravest mistakes of his life and seated Yonti and Shaya'le beside each other on the very same bench! What had prompted him to make such a blunder no one knew, for if there was one point on which all of Chasdei Moshe's members agreed unanimously, it was that Yonti and Shaya'le had to be placed as far apart as the shul's *mizrach* was from its back door. There were some who even ventured to say that there wasn't enough room for Shaya'le and Yonti in one shul, and that it would only be right to seat them in two separate shuls — provided, that is, that neither one of them was Chasdei Moshe.

That was because the two of them were thought to be too hard on their surroundings — and many times harder on each other.

Yonti was the contentious, intimidating one of the two. An unfortunate man, he worked for his living from dawn till dusk and had yet to see any blessing in his labor. Actually, it could be said that Yonti had never known a happy day in his life, a fact which caused many to wonder who was the jokester who had chosen to call him "Yom Tov," which means a "good day" in Hebrew.

Yonti made friends with no one, and, aside from the scathing condemnations he would occasionally hurl at one of the members of the shul, or at all of them collectively, he rarely grunted a sentence of more than two letters.

N and *O* being the letters he most frequently used.

Yonti extended to an unknown height and stretched across an unknown expanse of the same proportions. He was considered a giant, and his unusual measurements only reinforced his ominous image.

Yonti was rather humorless, to say the least. To tell the truth, claimed those in the know, when a sense of humor was being handed out, Yonti had been busy wrangling with someone on a different line and had missed getting his share. Groups close to those in the know claimed that the nameless "someone" had been none other than Shaya'le.

Shaya'le was Yonti's opposite — but not his complete opposite. He was small, short and so thin that when he skipped up the block there was always the fear that he might slip and fall through one of the many holes in his pants.

Shaya'le was also bit of a meddler, and there was no battle in the Chasdei Moshe shul — or in the dozens of other shuls in which he had *daven*ed before joining Chasdei Moshe — in which he hadn't had an arm or a leg and, according to those in the know, a nose.

Shaya'le was a skeptic, and one could always hear or see him grumbling and griping about someone or something. His eyes never focused on one point, because there was always another, more interesting, point which Shaya'le did not want to miss.

Fate had not been kind to Shaya'le either, taking him from job to job. He, too, was downtrodden and impoverished, and he, too, was burdened by a collection of tsuris as would make anyone bitter. But unlike reticent, ill-tempered Yonti, Shaya'le did not envelop himself in thundering silence or hide behind a scowling face. Instead, Shaya'le was in the habit of sending out through his mouth all those matters which irritated him. Since Shaya'le had a sharp tongue, these same matters came out in an especially caustic and biting manner.

Actually, Shaya'le was considered to have an exceptional sense of humor, and he was also accustomed to expelling his anger through the tunnel of this humor to his cutting tongue, which would then shred it into thin, sharp strips.

For a number of years, Yonti and Shaya'le barely knew each other, a fact which had been greeted with delight by the entire neighborhood — until the *gabbai* went and sat the two of them on the same bench.

৯ Chapter Two

The truth is that Yonti would never have noticed Shaya'le sitting next to him until this very day had there not been thrust directly under his nose a snuffbox whose rightful owner was none other then Shaya'le himself.

Yonti, you should know, also owned a snuffbox, but here the similarity ended. While Shaya'le would thrust his box in the face of anyone who owned a pair of nostrils, Yonti wasn't the type to offer anyone a snuffbox, or any kind of box at all, and whoever made the grave mistake of asking to sniff Yonti's snuff never did so again, because Yonti would extend his snuffbox with obvious reluctance, while emitting incomprehensible grunts which took away any pleasure in sniffing the snuff.

In Yonti's opinion, by thrusting his snuffbox at him in so sudden a manner, Shaya'le had grossly overstepped the bounds of propriety and good taste. As a matter of fact, most of the members of Chasdei Moshe agreed that Shaya'le was out of bounds on this point.

Yonti rose to his feet and prepared to teach Shaya'le a lesson in good manners. But just then, Shaya'le beat him to the punch and said, "No, you needn't bother offering me a sniff of your snuff, because your snuff sniffs from afar, and if I am not mistaken, you accidentally bought horse snuff."

In Yonti's opinion, this statement reflected Shaya'le's glaring lack of discernment, and he told him that he was certain that the snuff in his snuffbox was not for horses or any other kind of animal.

Truth be told, Shaya'le had not meant to offend Yonti but after the latter insinuated a lack of trustworthiness or knowledge on his part, Shaya'le decided to be stubborn and stick to his opinion that Yonti's snuff was of the horsy kind.

And that was their first argument.

From that Shabbos on, Shaya'le and Yonti would disagree on every subject in the world. Bench mates claimed that Yonti and Shaya'le had never — not even by mistake — agreed on a point.

One way or another, Yonti and Shaya'le became permanent adversaries, and the sounds of their arguments were heard from afar. Because of the halachah which prohibits speaking in shul, especially during prayers, Shaya'le and Yonti were forced to conduct their arguments afterwards, thus giving the entire street a chance to become familiar with the details of their opinions — especially the details of their opinions about each other.

Amazingly, neither of them ever took the trouble to express his opinion of the other behind his back. Yonti and Shaya'le's motto was, "The more the merrier," so their accusations against each other were always made face to face — facing each other, facing neighbors, facing buildings.

The arguments between the two became permanent and the pattern could be predicted in advance. Every time Shaya'le expressed a certain opinion on any topic under the sun (and Shaya'le was certainly used to expressing certain opinions on every topic under the sun), Yonti would dismiss it with a shake of his head or a wave of his hand. Sometimes Yonti would even venture to utter a few words of rebuttal.

In response, Shaya'le would aim his caustic tongue at Yonti and prove that his opinion was the correct one, and that Yonti's waves of the hand were nothing but empty gestures.

At this point, an argument, which would last for hours, would usually erupt, with each side attempting to find words sharp enough to prove the basic illogic of the other's opinion.

The years passed, something which certainly could not be said about the enmity of the two. That stayed the same, and even grew stronger with time. Actually, the whole neighborhood knew about it, and the numerous people who had tried to make peace between them failed abysmally. That's because each one of the pair explained in eloquently logical language why he simply could not stand the other. Their arguments were so convincing that the peacemakers, who anyway were not particularly fond of either of them, came to the conclusion that this conflict was irreconcilable due to the huge gap between the two.

Amongst themselves, those same peacemakers mused that it was probably better for both of them, and for the rest of the world as well. For as long as the two were busy with their arguing, at least others would be saved from harm.

It was on this premise that the efforts of the neighbors to make peace between the two grew fewer, and with nothing to disturb them, the two continued their argumentative, mud-slinging battles.

This arrangement lasted for fifteen years. The two rivals guarded their enmity zealously, and, actually, Chasdei Moshe grew famous — much to the credit, or perhaps due to the fault of, the two bitter adversaries in its midst.

❧ Chapter Three

When Yonti's daughter was about to get married, he told Shaya'le that he planned to celebrate her wedding at Gilah Gardens.

Shaya'le lost no time and lunged into a headlong assault against that wedding hall. "Everyone knows that the food they serve at Gilah Gardens isn't fresh, that the service is terrible and that the walls are peeling," claimed Shaya'le. "Go to Rinah Gates. That's the recommended place."

Yonti told Shaya'le that if he wanted to he could celebrate *his* daughter's wedding at Rinah Gates but that he, Yonti, had already reserved Gilah Gardens, which was known for its excellence.

Shaya'le, of course, had no intention of celebrating the wedding of his daughter in Gilah Gardens even once, because, among various reasons, to his dismay he did not have even one daughter for the life of him among his ten sons. And when he said this to Yonti, Yonti, who was blessed with eight daughters, declared that under no circumstances would he call any of them "for the life of him"!

But then, right at the height of the argument, what did Yonti do but stick his hand into his pocket and pull out an invitation to his daughter's wedding at Gilah Gardens!

Shaya'le was completely surprised by the unexpected invitation from his confirmed adversary but he didn't lose his head and murmured, "Even though Gilah Gardens is still, at this very moment, the worst hall in town, I'll restrain myself and come to the wedding." With this, of course, the argument about the quality of the hall and its service resumed even more vigorously, and one of the stormiest quarrels in the annals of the two was recorded for posterity.

Of course, the members of Chasdei Moshe were very surprised when they saw Shaya'le and his entire family at the wedding of Yonti's daughter. One congregant even dared ask Shaya'le what he was doing there, to which Shaya'le replied that he didn't understand the question. After all, doesn't he sit next to Yonti in shul?

The members of the shul were doubly surprised when Yonti was honored with one of the *sheva berachos* under the *chuppah* of Shaya'le's son (which, by the way, took place at Gilah Gardens, even though Yonti had claimed that after his daughter's wedding he had become convinced that at the time, Shaya'le had been right, and that the hall was indeed musty and horrible. But Shaya'le admitted to him that it was because of that same wedding that he was finally convinced that Yonti had been right at the time when he said it was an excellent hall, although he qualified his words and declared that Yonti should by no means jump to the conclusion that he was right about other things as well but only about this particular matter, and that was all!)

On this topic, too, a vociferous argument erupted between the two, one which convinced the members of Chasdei Moshe that Shaya'le's honoring Yonti with a *berachah* at his daughter's wedding and Yonti's inviting Shaya'le to his son's wedding had been one-time slip-ups, and that the two hated each other more than ever.

❧ Chapter Four

One *erev Shabbos*, a strange silence emanated from Yonti and Shaya'le's bench.

Members of the shul who turned around to see what had happened quickly discovered that Yonti hadn't come to shul. Shaya'le sat in his place, obviously very worried.

"What happened to Yonti?" they asked him.

"He's in the hospital," replied Shaya'le. "What? You don't know? I always yelled at him to stop eating so much but that wise guy always has to do the opposite of what I tell him, and now he's hospitalized in intensive care because of a terrible heart attack."

This news frightened the members of Chasdei Moshe. Most of them called Yonti's home after Shabbos to send him wishes for a speedy recovery. A few of them made the effort to visit Yonti in the intensive care unit.

Those who took the trouble to visit Yonti pointed out two important facts to their fellow congregants. The first fact was that the attack on Yonti's heart was indeed massive and nearly fatal. The second fact was that a certain person sat beside Yonti's bed all the time, fighting and arguing with him. Who was this person if none other than his perennial adversary, Shaya'le?

Those visitors charged the hospital staff with negligence in letting Shaya'le enter Yonti's room at so critical a time, because Yonti's weak heart might undergo another attack, *chalilah*, at the mere sight of his long-standing enemy. Actually, the doctors also thought so when they saw the two arguing, and in the beginning had even sent Shaya'le away, saying that Yonti was in critical condition and it was forbidden for him to get angry. But from the minute Shaya'le left, Yonti's situation deteriorated, and at his request, Shaya'le was summoned back to the hospital. Yonti claimed that Shaya'le had called him back because he had a winning answer to Shaya'le's argument. Shaya'le heard Yonti's rebuttal and told him that it had been very unfair to get someone out of bed for so ridiculous a reply, and thus the argument proceeded as usual.

Apparently, Shaya'le took advantage of every available opportunity to visit Yonti. So frequent were his visits that his employer told him that, if he wanted, he'd get him some kind of a job in the hospital, because this hobby of his seemed to conflict with his regular work schedule.

One night, Shaya'le sat beside Yonti's bed, feeding him some soup. Between spoonfuls, the two conducted a raging argument, each one berating and insulting the other in a particularly sharp manner.

Suddenly, strangely, their arguing ceased. An eerie and thundering silence prevailed between them.

Shaya'le continued to feed Yonti wordlessly. Each was engrossed in his thoughts.

"Yonti," Shaya'le said at last in a voice more tremulous than usual.

"Yes, Shaya'le," Yonti replied.

"I wanted to ask you," spoke Shaya'le. "Perhaps you could let me sniff your snuff?"

Yonti, surprised, looked through his drawer and took out the box of snuff which Shaya'le had never in his life sniffed.

With a trembling hand, he lifted the lid and thrust it under Shaya'le's nose. Shaya'le inhaled a deep sniff and looked Yonti squarely in the eye. He seemed to see a tear forming.

Shaya'le discovered a bit of moisture in Yonti's eyes.

In an instant, they both realized that all those years, they had been one heart, one soul. Suddenly, they fell on each other's necks.

"Yonti," Shaya'le was heard saying, "your snuff really does smell like horses."

Oy, such enemies!

Agon's Secret

The sun was sinking on the horizon. The old tombstones in the neglected cemetery of Warsaw were bathed in brilliant orange. Gently, the sun, the only guest which visited the cemetery regularly, caressed the tombstones hiding tumultuous sagas of yore. Now it too was about to disappear. Only one person was seen in the large cemetery, and he was a stranger, wearing a tailored suit and a black felt hat.

The man stood, his eyes widening as he gazed at the two tombstones nearest him.

Anyone casting even a casual glance at him would have noticed the unrestrained shock, surprise and rage drawn across his face. There was, however, no one to cast that glance, save for one elderly man of about ninety, who, resting on his cane, slowly neared the plot on which the stranger was standing, until he stood right next to it.

"Can you explain the meaning of this?" asked the stranger angrily, pointing to the two nearest tombstones. On one of them was inscribed, "HaRav Yechiel Reizner, *z"l*," and on the other was written, "Aharon Shreiber, *z"l*."

"What is there for me to explain?" asked the old man in surprise. "Is there a mistake in the inscription on one, or perhaps both?"

"No, not at all," the stranger hastened to explain. "But pray tell, why was Aharon Shreiber, that hard, ill-mannered man called 'Agon' by everyone, buried right next to my father, Reb Yechiel *z"l*, who so objected to him during his lifetime?"

In order to understand the reason for his indignation, we must go back in time. We must tell a story which unfolded forty years earlier, not long before the stranger, Michael Reizner, took leave of his family and made *aliyah* to *Eretz HaKodesh*.

❧ Chapter Two

It was the most ordinary of days, that day forty years ago, when suddenly Warsaw's Schwimmel Lane was abuzz with a rumor that Reb Yechiel had declared that he would never again step foot in Agon's grocery.

Naturally, this rumor sent shock waves throughout the neighborhood, since Reb Yechiel was considered a learned, respected personality who had never in his life resorted to this type of measure. Nevertheless, everyone well understood Reb Yechiel and even loudly congratulated him for his decision.

Reb Yechiel was apparently thoroughly convinced that Agon, who was in his eyes incapable of running even a lumberyard, was certainly not qualified to operate a grocery serving all of Schwimmel Lane's residents.

No matter how one looked at him, Agon appeared, and even sounded, like a hardhearted man. He was tall, and his shoulders supported a face not likely to cause children to smile or to remain on the same side of the lane when they saw him approaching.

Agon was in his fifties and always looked and sounded angry. In the morning, he would growl at the milkmen and later on, at the customers who arrived before he had finished putting the store in order, then at the youngsters who pushed the elderly, and, after that, at the oldsters who, he felt, pestered him.

Unlike a different type of person who locks his anger and complaints inside his heart, which serves him in effect as a kind of storage room, Agon's outspokenness was directed against every group and faction living in Schwimmel Lane, and he tried to take care of each and every one of them personally, in the name of justice and conscience.

There was no argument — and on this even his fiercest opponents agreed — that of all the hovels in Warsaw which served as grocery stores, Agon's was the neatest and cleanest. Once he had even received a framed certificate from the government, attesting to the order and cleanliness of his store. But what did Agon do but take the special certificate out of its frame and wrap Mr. Reisenbach's milk in it? And what did he do if not put his price list in the frame?

To those who were curious about his actions, Agon explained that his store needed no certificate — something he could under no circumstances say about the frame.

One way or another, Agon continued to spew forth a barrage of complaints and accusations against every object or human being who moved within his range of vision. Likewise, he never neglected people or objects which didn't move, or which did but not in his range of vision.

In the end, a large group of opponents formed from various factions in Schwimmel Lane and decided unanimously that it was inconceivable to continue doing business with a nuisance like Agon, and that all the residents must stop patronizing his store until he would be forced to close.

❧ *Chapter Three*

At first, Reb Yechiel had opposed taking so drastic a step. However, when the pressure increased, he turned towards Agon's store and asked to speak with him about this and that.

Agon asked Reb Yechiel if the main part of the conversation was about this or mostly about that. When there was no reply from Reb Yechiel, Agon told him, "Can't you see that I don't have any time now? There are customers. Do me a favor — don't block the scenery."

This comment, of course, did not do much to enhance or diminish Reb Yechiel's prestige. That was because the only view in Agon's store was the old icebox, and even if we were to take a very kindly approach to this same box, there was no way it could be called "scenery."

But Reb Yechiel wanted to clarify the matter thoroughly, so, like one of the empty bottles standing in Agon's store, he waited for Agon to approach him.

When the last customer had finished his business, Agon turned to Reb Yechiel with a pointed question: "*Nu?*"

"People complain that you don't treat the residents of the neighborhood with respect," said Reb Yechiel.

"Correct," Agon admitted happily. "So what?"

"Why?" asked Reb Yechiel.

"I sell milk, not respect," answered Agon.

Reb Yechiel peered at Agon's face and tried to detect the trace of a smirk. Agon's face, though, was as serious as could be.

"People are liable to think that you are rude," said Reb Yechiel.

"And what if I really am?" asked Agon.

To that Reb Yechiel had no reply. He took a deep breath and said to Agon, "You should know that if you don't change your ways, I'll stop patronizing your store!"

"Did I ever ask you to shop here?" asked Agon incredulously. Then he added, "Perhaps I'm not nice by nature. Perhaps the anger inside me causes me to be rude. In any case, I have no intention of feigning even one extra smile, because I am no hypocrite. Likewise, I have no intention of keeping my criticisms about this and that locked inside me for the same reason."

"Why are you so angry?" asked Reb Yechiel.

"That's none of your business," replied Agon. "Now, let me close *my* business."

That was the end of the conversation between Reb Yechiel and Agon. The next day came Reb Yechiel's announcement that he would no longer patronize Agon's store.

The truth is, Reb Yechiel didn't ask anyone else to follow his example. However, Reb Yechiel's stature in the neighborhood was so solid that many imitated him, and within two months, nearly everyone had forsaken Agon's grocery store and begun to shop at the grocer in the next neighborhood.

All this took place forty years prior to the conversation between the old man and Michael. During that period, Michael Reizner, Reb Yechiel's son, had taken leave of his family and emigrated to *Eretz HaKodesh*.

Since then, he had heard absolutely nothing about Agon and, as a matter of fact, nothing about the members of his very own family, except that the cursed Holocaust had wiped them out, along with six million other Jews.

Now, when he came to visit the graves of his family forty years later and found his father's tombstone right next to Agon's, it was no wonder he recalled that difficult individual and had pointed to the tombstones angrily, asking the old man, "What is the meaning of this?"

❧ *Chapter Four*

"Calm down," the man told him. "Listen to the rest of the story, and let me tell you what happened after you left."

As the old man spoke, he leaned on his cane and told Michael the rest of the story.

It seems that Agon wasn't bothered by the fact that most of the neighborhood's residents boycotted his store, and he continued to rise before dawn every day to arrange his shelves, together with his loyal assistant Yonasan Rothstein, and to scowl at those customers who still, for some reason, continued to come.

It should be mentioned that Agon had much less work now because he had many times fewer supplies to arrange than what he was used to. Despite this, Agon told anyone who was ready to listen that his store would remain open, even if he himself would be its only customer.

Slowly, all of the customers deserted Agon's store, and throughout most of the day, Agon and his loyal assistant, Yonasan Rothstein, would sit at the entrance, arms folded, doing nothing.

When Yonasan began to feel that he was eating bread of charity from Agon's living flesh, he notified him that he was leaving, not out of anger or disloyalty but rather because he knew that Agon didn't need him and had no means to pay him his salary. Customers were hardly seen in the store, and even Agon had nothing to do most hours of the day.

Agon nodded his head sadly, put an arm on his assistant's shoulder and said, "Go, Yonasan. Take care of yourself." Afterwards, as if on second thought, he added, "But I warn you, don't say a thing." He had no need to say more. Yonasan was fully aware of the secret he was forbidden to reveal.

Actually, Yonasan's resignation was a mere formality. In truth, he continued to sit next to Agon every day and watch all the people rushing towards the grocery store in the next neighborhood.

They would sit together and look at each other. Agon never admitted that he had been hurt. On the contrary, he repeatedly told Yonasan that the people who had stopped coming to his store had done him a favor, because now he had time to rest. But Yonasan, who knew his employer better than anyone else, knew so well how much blood poured out of his wounded heart.

Half a year went by when a rumor passed through the Lane that Meir, one of Agon's chief antagonists, had been seen shopping in Agon's store on the sly.

The shocking piece of news had barely been digested when it was reported that dozens of other customers had also been spied slinking into Agon's store to buy groceries.

If the truth be told, the source of these rumors was none other than Yonasan Rothstein, Agon's loyal assistant. When Yonasan saw how some of Agon's foes were returning to him, he began to circulate the rumor among the Lane's residents that "they're beginning to come back to Agon."

❧ Chapter Five

All this was surprising and rather puzzling. No one understood why those very people who had opposed Agon so openly were going back to his store — or why they hid it from the other residents of the Lane.

The rumors reached Reb Yechiel's ears in no time at all, and he asked someone to call Meir, who had been one of Agon's staunchest adversaries — actually the one who more than anyone else had convinced him to stop shopping in Agon's store.

"Why did you go back to shopping in his store?" Reb Yechiel asked Meir.

Meir blushed and stammered, "I can't go on shopping in the other neighborhood anymore."

"Why not?" Reb Yechiel asked.

"I'll tell you," Meir replied. "At the end of the first month after I left Agon's store, I went to the competing grocer to pay the bill, only to discover to my shock that I needed to pay a sum twice or even three times more than what I was used to paying at Agon's.

"I went over to the grocer and complained about the big bill but he proved to me that what I had bought totaled that amount. At first, I thought I must have bought too much, so I decided to cut down on my purchases. Next month, though, my bill was almost the same, as it was the following month, too.

"From then on, I began to pay in cash, since I owed at the store. To do so, I was forced to borrow money, because I simply didn't have enough. In the end, the bill I paid was only slightly less than that of the previous month.

"Several months passed like that, and now I have no one to borrow from. I can't buy on credit either, because I still owe money to the grocer. That's why there's no choice — in order not to die of starvation, I came back to Agon's store."

It seemed strange to Reb Yechiel. That's why he asked a few other people to come, and from all of them he heard similar stories.

Reb Yechiel was very surprised. He himself found no difference between the sums he had paid in Agon's store and those he paid in the store in the next neighborhood. Besides, he was absolutely sure that the groceries in the new store were not more expensive than those of Agon's store.

The mystery perplexed Reb Yechiel and bothered a great deal. That's why he summoned Yonasan Rothstein, Agon's assistant, and began to question him. When he saw that Yonasan was evading his questions, he said to him, "I demand that you explain why the prices of the two stores are so different."

Yonasan looked here and there, and at last he said, "I cannot remain silent any longer. I'll tell you everything.

"You should know," Yonasan intoned, "that every month, when I reviewed the store's ledgers, Agon would stand beside me and erase sizable amounts from the accounts of dozens of customers who, in his opinion, were unable to support their families. Most of those whose debts were erased were Torah scholars or *kollel* students who found it hard to provide for their large families. But there were others, too, who to all outward appearances seemed well-off but who, as Agon had found out in his own way, were not.

"Agon warned me not to dare reveal this. He threatened to fire me if he found out I had told. But now that I don't work for him, I feel I have a right to tell all."

Reb Yechiel buried his head in his hands for quite some time. At last, he turned to Yonasan and asked, "About what is Agon so angry all these years? Why does he act that way on the outside when he has a heart of gold?"

Yonasan shrugged. "I don't know. The one and only time he said something that might explain anything was when I asked him why he scorned everyone while secretly doing *chesed* for them. He only told me, 'There are people who are by nature cross and ill-tempered, and their temperament is not pleasant. But are they forbidden to do mitzvos?' "

Reb Yechiel parted from Yonasan. "That's all I need to know," he said.

❧ Chapter Six

Two days later, Reb Yechiel visited Agon's store. He waited until the few customers had finished their shopping, and after that, Agon's store closed, leaving Reb Yechiel and Agon sitting inside talking.

For four hours Reb Yechiel and Agon sat inside the store and talked. At the end of four hours, when Reb Yechiel left the store, his eyes were red and he was muttering, "This poor, unfortunate man is a *tzaddik*," and other enigmatic comments.

The next day, Reb Yechiel began to shop at Agon's store again and with him, the residents of the Lane who used to shop there.

They returned to Agon not only to shop but also to hear his scolding and to listen to his opinions about anyone in general, and everyone in particular. Only now, for some reason, not a single person grumbled about him or his complaints.

Had the truth seeped into their ears at last, as is the way of all truth in crowded lanes? Or was it Reb Yechiel's remarks to one resident of the Lane?

And what had Reb Yechiel said? Listen carefully:

"Anger over a loss has an element of love, for if you don't love something, you aren't angry over it's loss. Agon loved and loves Torah study and its scholars, and because of that, he's angry that he has no share in it. For that reason, he speaks gruffly to them — not out of animosity but out of love."

Life returned to normal, and to the long list of people and organizations against whom Agon railed was added another name — Yonasan Rothstein — because he had revealed the secret to Reb Yechiel.

Agon began to call him "a character who can't be trusted," as well a variety of other unflattering descriptions he had become expert in over the years. Although he re-hired him, he continued to tell anyone who was willing to listen what he thought of him.

But do you think that Yonasan Rothstein was offended by all this? Not in the least. He was delighted and unfazed by the names hurled at him. As far as he was concerned, these remarks were indications of the health and strength of the angry man with the heart of gold whom Yonasan knew and admired more than anyone else — Agon.

The sun had already set. A chill wind blew through the old cemetery of Warsaw. The old man finished his story, and Michael Reizner stood, deep in thought, continuing to wipe away the tears which had been streaming from his eyes the entire time.

"Now do you understand why your father asked in his will to be buried next to Agon, who died a year before him?" asked the old man.

Michael remained riveted to the ground, still as a stone.

"I understand," he spoke at last. "I certainly do understand."

The old man placed his hand gently on Michael's shoulder and said, "Don't worry. Your father merited to be buried beside a charitable man. Next to hidden *tzaddik*." Then he turned around and began to walk heavily towards the exit.

Suddenly, Michael awoke from his reverie and called out to the old man. "How did you hear this story? Did you know my father or Agon, may they rest in peace? Did you ever talk to them?"

The old man turned around and smiled. "Did I forget to tell you? My name is Yonasan Rothstein."

The Old Man
and the
Sea

Although his real name is Yirmeyahu, no one called him that. Most everyone called him "the Old Man and the Sea," and not just most people but even Yirmeyahu himself.

The most popular version of the story about how he got that name is that the Russian youths he taught on a voluntary basis were the ones responsible for the strange nickname but that Cymbel, a neighbor, also played an important role. Woe to anyone who tries to deny Cymbel that credit — or any other credit due him.

Cymbel, it seems, had heard the Russian youths calling Yirmeyahu "*dadushka moreh*," a combination of Russian and Hebrew meaning, "Grandpa the teacher." But Cymbel, not being a man of complexity, went and asked one of the Russians who knew Hebrew what "*dadushke*" meant.

"Grandpa," came the reply.

"And what does the word *'moreh'* mean in Russian?" he asked further.

"Sea," came the answer.

Cymbel walked around in a daze for an entire day. "Grandpa Sea," he kept repeating, when suddenly from the depths of his memory arose the title of a book he had once heard about many years ago, *The Old Man and the Sea*, a book written by a journalist named Hemingway or something. *This was surely what they meant*, the thought came to him.

From that time on, the eighty-year-old Yirmeyahu was called "the Old Man and the Sea."

There were differing opinions regarding Yirmeyahu's ripe old age. There were those who claimed that he had begun counting his years from the age of eight. Others countered that a man as intelligent as Yirmeyahu surely knew how to count by the age of five. On one point they all agreed: the Old Man and the Sea was a remarkable character. He was a wise and beloved old man, who enthralled everyone — adults, adolescents and children.

He spoke a beautiful, correct Hebrew. "I was a teacher for sixty years," he answered apologetically when asked about it. Actually, the Old Man and the Sea never stopped being a teacher. He so loved his occupation, that whenever there was an opportunity, he continued to teach.

When the Russians began arriving in Israel, his large, empty house filled with children and teenagers who came to him so that he could tutor them for free. He helped them prepare their homework, corrected their mistakes and told them exciting stories. Yes, he spoke Russian, as well as seven other languages.

The Old Man and the Sea had no problem making contact with people. He would begin with "good morning," then stroke the cheek of a baby in a carriage, and in a matter of moments become one of the family, an adopted grandfather.

He was very meticulous about his dress. It should be mentioned, though, that although each one of the items in his wardrobe was quite nice by itself, their combination on the body of one man, especially one with about eighty years behind him, was a little bit extraordinary. It wasn't surprising to see him appear wearing a blue necktie with a plaid shirt, and over it a yellow jacket to match his green pants.

No one ever called the Old Man and the Sea "Abba."

Only after a few conjectures here and there was the explanation heard that the Old Man and the Sea had once had a son. But he wasn't willing to say a thing about it, and his neighbors respected that wish.

The Old Man and the Sea was invited to a different home every Shabbos, and really, there was such a long line of people waiting to invite him that he would never have been able to accept them all unless he lived to be 120. In order not to disappoint anyone, the Old Man and the Sea used to tell people that he had no intention of moving to a new apartment after the age of one hundred and twenty but instead planned on living in the neighborhood until he got *really* old.

Families who reached the top of the list enjoyed a very interesting Shabbos. The stories he told never ended. And considering his eighty and some odd years, why should they? A Shabbos with him was especially exciting — that's why his hosts usually invited additional relatives and friends to enjoy it as well.

On one such *Shabbos*, the Berger family eagerly awaited his visit... but he never came.

Usually the Old Man and the Sea was very prompt. Neighborhood experts in such matters claimed that he was the only person in the world who arrived at a wedding or bar mitzvah precisely at the time written on the invitation. Knowing this, the Bergers worried that something terrible might have happened to him.

Reb Moishe, the father of the family, rushed over to the old man's home but to his surprise, found him sitting and dining with a silver-haired stranger who spoke a broken Hebrew.

Before he could get a word out of his mouth, the old man said, "Sit down, Reb Moishe. Please meet my son, Reuven, or Robert, as he calls himself. Forgive me for having disappointed you. He arrived on Friday only a few minutes before Shabbos, and I was so excited that I forgot to tell you that I wouldn't be coming."

This earthshaking news completely removed any of the disappointment Reb Moishe felt. However, he quickly recovered and in an authoritative tone told the old man and his son, "Both of you are coming to my house right now."

Obviously Robert, the son of the Old Man and the Sea, wasn't accustomed to such commands, and surely no one had ever attempted to kidnap him from his home, especially since Robert was not the type of person anyone would want to kidnap. That's why Robert looked around the room, searching perhaps for a weapon with which to ward off the attacker who had barged into his father's house. But to his surprise, his father rose and said to him, "Reuven, let's go."

To make a long story short, Reb Moishe took the frail hand of the Old Man and the Sea and led him to his house, while Mr. Robert trailed behind.

Robert suffered his second shock when he sat down for the Shabbos meal, especially after it was explained to him that the twenty-seven people seated around Reb Moishe's table belonged to only three families. Even though it was evident that Robert knew nothing about Judaism, he was an expert in multiplication and division, being a successful accountant in Los Angeles. A simple calculation proved to him that each family consisted of about nine members, and Robert had never seen nor heard of a family that had more than two children and one pet.

He happened to enjoy the noise and commotion. The children turned out to be very friendly or, to be more exact, overly friendly. Robert proved to be an easily climbable object and didn't utter a peep even when several children climbed on him all at once. Reb Moshe's wife and others in the family still claim that Robert did utter a few peeps of protest but they weren't heard — and why should they be?

The minute Robert's father began to speak, the children rushed to their parents and waited to hear every word of the Old Man and the Sea. But for the first time in his life, and in the lives of his listeners, the Old Man and the Sea found it hard to find the right words.. The guests were touched. A few tension-filled moments passed.

"I have already told you," the old man finally said, "that I arrived here when I was forty-two. What I hadn't yet told you is that my two children were with me. One fell ill from the hardships of the journey and died when we arrived, and the second one is Reuven, who now calls himself Robert. We came straight to this neighborhood, although it would be hard to call a shack in the middle of an orange grove a neighborhood. That's when I made an enormous, terrible mistake. Having been a teacher all my life, I decided that it was inconceivable to send my son, Reuven, to a religious school, because the ones nearby then were inadequate and poorly funded. I decided that nothing would happen if I sent my son to public school, where he would learn science and general studies. 'I'll teach him religion myself,' I said.

"I'll skip the unpleasant details. I'll say only this: Reuven grew and continued to study in public school. He removed his head-covering and left the country. The ties between us were severed when in the end, he married a non-Jewish woman.

"That's why you never heard about him. You know me as a teacher and an educator," said the Old Man and the Sea, tears forming in his eyes, "but I failed abysmally with the education of my own son. I admit my guilt."

At this point, the guests refrained from looking at Robert, who sat huddled in his corner, his head in his hands, nodding at his father's every word.

Suddenly Robert rose and straightened his shoulders. "Do you think I succeeded in life? Not in the least. Today I am sixty-five. Twenty years ago, I divorced my gentile wife. True, I am very rich but I have no family or friends. Imagine, then, how I feel, coming here and seeing my father, the man I sought to run away from my whole life, surrounded by so many loving friends. Now I am beginning to feel all too well how my good years were spent in sorrow, in a strange land, surrounded by strangers. I have no one to blame but myself for wasting my life. Not only did I lose out on a family and friends, I also lost out on a life of truth, on Judaism!"

"Reuven," someone cried out from the corner of the room.

Everyone looked in the direction of the voice. "Reuven, do you remember me?" The speaker was none other than the father of Reb Moishe Berger, a bearded Jew about Robert's age.

"No."

"I'm Yosef Berger. We were in the same class together in school — don't you remember?"

Robert stood up, look at Yosef and murmured, "I don't believe it! Is it really you?"

"You still haven't lost your life," said Yosef. "True, you have lost a part of it but you still have a long time left in which to be happy. I also grew up non-religious. I served in the underground and became far removed from religion. But in the merit of one man I did complete *teshuvah* — and look at the family I've raised.

"Do you know who the man was who changed my life?" Yosef Berger asked Robert. "That man is sitting next to you." He pointed to the person sitting beside Robert.

And to whom did Yosef Berger point if not to the bowed figure of the Old Man and the Sea?

Reb Shmuel
Builds a
Sukkah

E very year, right after Yom Kippur, Reb
Shmuel Eisner would begin building a sukkah
outside the small neighborhood synagogue he
attended.

He lived in a quiet, dreary neighborhood, most of
whose residents were not Torah- or mitzvah-observant. The
small synagogue, which had known better years, was no
longer grand and was now rarely visited.

The few observant Jews in the neighborhood built
their sukkahs in their yards or on the roofs of their homes,
while those who were distanced from Torah saw no point in
putting up the temporary structure and made do with furtive
glances at those of their neighbors.

The various types of residents in the neighborhood
had nothing in common except for one subject on which all
agreed: Everyone felt that Reb Shmuel Eisner's building of
the sukkah next to the synagogue was backbreaking, pur-

poseless work since, except for stray cats who took shelter in it now and then, there was not a single person alive who gave it as much as a glance. Actually, those in the know went to the trouble of pointing out that even the cats were doing Reb Shmuel a big favor in displaying an interest in his sukkah, and also noted that they did so only on rainy days.

One of the neighborhood jesters actually suggested to Reb Shmuel that he put a roof over the structure so that the cats could have a real shelter from the rain. Reb Shmuel sincerely explained to him, though, that this would be impossible because, according to halachah, one may not cover a sukkah with a roof.

❧ Chapter Two: The Ceremonies

The neighbors grew accustomed to seeing Reb Shmuel, together with his sons, lug the old, heavy boards out of the storage room and put them together to make a sukkah.

It was really a pitiful sight, they felt, to see Reb Shmuel's sons straining to drag those boards and stand them up. The children were young, and the old fashioned boards of real wood were heavy and cumbersome. The boards were held together by various bolts and screws, and each board had its traditional place. One mistake in place-ment and the entire architectural creation would turn into a pile of wood. Actually, many of the neighbors thought that the company which manufactured those boards should have been outlawed, and that its directors should be incarcerated for life. Reb Shmuel did not agree — especially since the factory owner had given him the boards for free.

One way or the other, the building of the sukkah took quite a few long hours of work and was accompanied by quite a few admonishments and instructions from Reb Shmuel to his sons. The admonishments were varied and sharp, and to someone looking on from the sidelines it would seem that those young children ought to be pitied for having such a man for a father. However, the children, for some strange reason, seemed happy and content, and would regale each other gleefully with the latest tease they had gotten.

Even more curious was the second ceremony, which took place after the process of construction was almost completed. When the last screws were about to be given their final turn, Reb Shmuel would invariably say, "If you've come here to waste your time, you might as well go home. I'll do the work myself." That was always the sign that the sukkah was finished. The children would then return home, and a few minutes later, their father would join them.

During those moments, Reb Shmuel would hang a sign which read, "Let all those who are hungry come and eat," and to anyone who pointed out to him that the sign was really more appropriate for Pesach, he would answer firmly, "Yes, also for Pesach."

The neighbors were convinced that Reb Shmuel's strange compulsion to build a sukkah which no one needed was being passed down to his sons — but there was nothing they could do about it.

❧ Chapter Three: Mishkin

From the second year of building the sukkah on, Reb Shmuel developed the habit of knocking on the door of Mr. Mishkin, opposite whose window grew an impressive palm tree.

Mr. Mishkin was known as "the Communist." That's what he was called by all the neighbors who had become accustomed over the years to his favorable opinions of the Communist regime. Actually, the neighbors claimed that Reb Shmuel had found the last person in the world who would want to give even a moment's thought to that same structure which he built once a year next to the synagogue, for Mr. Mishkin's views were devoid of any trace of religion. According to the neighbors, anyone could see that Reb Shmuel lacked even a minimal understanding of human nature by the very fact that he had asked "the Communist" to let him cut fronds from the palm tree outside his private living-room window.

And, indeed, the first time Reb Shmuel approached Mr. Mishkin with his request he received a frosty welcome, for Mr. Mishkin thought it totally unjustified to cut off a branch from a tree for the sake of an "ancient custom."

After a torrent of unsavory and negative remarks about Reb Shmuel himself and the religion he believed in, the Communist told him, "There happen to be a few branches which I had thought to cut off anyway because they are blocking my view. I don't mind if you want to do the work for free instead of me having to pay for it."

In that manner, Reb Shmuel obtained beautiful *sechach* for his sukkah.

Once the sukkah was erected, Reb Shmuel would adorn it with the most exquisite and costly decorations imaginable, until it was even more beautiful than his own.

A sukkah there was, decorations as well, but of visitors, there were none. During the entire week of the holiday, the sukkah remained empty and abandoned. Nary a guest was seen inside it, and passersby would nod their heads in sorrow, pitying Reb Shmuel's wasted efforts.

Nevertheless, it became apparent that someone did visit it, and this could be deduced from the many decorations which were taken down from their places and actually stolen from the sukkah. Reb Shmuel, in the opinion of the neighbors, was left stripped, not only of the energy he invested but also of the mitzvah he wanted to have — not to mention the decorations.

The next year, Reb Shmuel again built a sukkah. The members of the synagogue advised Reb Shmuel to build a door for the sukkah, so that at least the decorations would remain intact. But Reb Shmuel answered them, "I build a sukkah so that people will be able to visit it at all times of the day, and if I lock it, no one will be able to enter."

The claims of the congregants that the cats would manage to enter it come what may, fell on deaf ears.

That year, too, Reb Shmuel visited the Communist and knocked on his door. Again he was greeted by a barrage of opprobrium and scorn and was barely permitted to cut the few branches which concealed Mr. Mishkin's view.

The scene repeated itself year after year. Reb Shmuel's sons were growing older and had begun to study in yeshivos. Some had even gotten married. Nonetheless, they found time, once a year, to help their father carry the heavy boards, to join them together the right way, to listen to his teasing, and, of course, to be sent home a minute before the completion of the work because of their laziness.

After all, that was part of their tradition, wasn't it?

The theft of the decorations continued. That, too, was a kind of tradition.

❧ Chapter Four: The Thief

Mr. Mishkin, the Communist, was growing older; Reb Shmuel also showed signs of his age. Only the palm tree remained as fresh as ever, managing to sprout a number of branches which concealed Mr. Mishkin's view in order to enable him to permit their cutting — not of course before offering the usual measure of scorn and abuse.

In that respect at least, the Communist showed no signs of aging.

Thirty years had passed since the sukkah was built for the first time. Thirty years of loneliness and neglect had been its lot, something which could not be said about its decorations. And then came the Sukkos which produced one of the most moving dramas ever to unfold in the neighborhood, and perhaps the most moving of them all.

On the third day of *Chol HaMoed Sukkos*, at midnight, the tranquillity of the neighborhood was suddenly disturbed by a police siren. The residents of the peaceful neighborhood poked their heads out of their windows to see what was happening and saw a very strange sight indeed.

Two policemen had surrounded Reb Shmuel's neglected sukkah were calling out into it. And who do you think emerged from it, frightened and dismayed, if not Mr. Mishkin, the Communist!

"At last we've caught the person who's been stealing the decorations," cried the neighbor who had summoned the police. "Every year decorations are stolen from here, and this year I decided to stay awake to catch the thief. I heard a noise and saw a figure crouched inside. I didn't wait even a minute — I called the police immediately," he declared proudly.

Meanwhile, dozens of neighbors, among them Reb Shmuel, arrived and encircled the policemen who were holding the confused and frightened Mr. Mishkin. "Who would have believed that he is a thief?" they whispered.

"Leave him alone," Reb Shmuel's voice was heard.

"We have to take him in for questioning," the policemen said, and they started to take Mr. Mishkin with them.

"Release him this instant," ordered Reb Shmuel in a voice which was not his. "He is not the thief."

"And who are you?" the policemen asked him.

✑ Chapter Five: Reb Shmuel's Story

"I'll tell you," said Reb Shmuel. "My name is Shmuel Eisner. I was born in Russia in an out-of-the-way place. The village in which I lived had a small Jewish community. It was in the time of the czar, before the Communist Revolution. My father, a prominent rabbi, was quite ill. Even standing up was hard for him. He spent most of his days at home, studying Torah and issuing halachic rulings.

"Every year, right after Yom Kippur, one of the members of the community, a man named Shlomo Zalman, would arrive at our house, together with his son, a young boy who was older than I by a couple of years, and the two would build our sukkah without saying a word.

"I remember that I became friends with that boy. I hung around and tried to help. But the two of them were stronger and faster than I was. The son would help his father and was repaid, in turn, with criticism and teasing.

"Right before the completion of the sukkah, the father would always say to his son that because he was so lazy he could go home. The boy would flash me a shy smile and leave. One time I went with him and tried to bolster his spirits. 'I saw you work so hard,' I told him. 'Your father's only saying that.'

"He burst out laughing. 'You may not know it but I come just to hear my father's teasing. It's a kind of humor that I don't get to hear the rest of the year, for only when he's building the sukkah does this special, lighthearted mood come over my father. I just love it.'"

Reb Shmuel paused for a moment, and the entire crowd stood open-mouthed, their eyes riveted on him. They understood that this wasn't just a simple story but one which contained hidden meaning. So enthralled were they by the story that they forgot to look in Mr. Mishkin's direction and therefore didn't notice that cold and distant man now silently weeping.

"One year I saw Reb Shlomo Zalman whisper a few words into my father's ear. Right after that my father took me aside to a secret corner and ordered me not to speak with Reb Shlomo Zalman's son about anything ever again. He refused to say more than that, and I understood that this command was made because of what Reb Shlomo Zalman had told my father.

"I didn't speak with the boy. I didn't even accompany him when he was sent home at the end. Years later, I found out that the boy had been ensnared by the ideological cult called 'Communism' which believed in equality between rich and poor, as well as the abolition of all religion. A few years later, the Communist Revolution took place, and harsh decrees were enacted against us. My father died there, in exile, and I barely managed to emigrate to *Eretz Yisrael*.

"The first time I built the sukkah, I thought that many of the neighborhood's residents would come," Reb Shmuel continued. "However, I was mistaken. Instead, I even became the target of ridicule. Towards the end of that Sukkos, I decided not to build another sukkah next to the synagogue.

"But on the night before Hoshana Rabbah, I happened to pass by the synagogue and hear noises emanating from the sukkah. I moved closer and peered through one of the cracks.

"And who did I see inside, humming quietly to himself, if not that same youth, the son of Reb Shlomo Zalman Mishkin?"

A wail was heard, and the tear-filled eyes of the crowd turned towards Mr. Mishkin, who sat on the ground, half sobbing, half listening to Reb Shmuel's story.

"Even then I knew that I had to repay Reb Shlomo Zalman for the many favors he had done for my father. I decided to build a sukkah every year for his son, the one who got caught up with a bad crowd, the one who used to creep inside my sukkah every year to remind and reawaken him."

And then, in front of everyone, the old Communist strode toward Reb Shmuel, touched his face, looked at him, and whispered: "Shmelke Eisner, who would have believed...?"

The two clasped hands and wept. The scene was beyond the comprehension of those present — because it was sad, because it was happy... and because it was unlike any other scene they had ever witnessed in their lives.

✌ The End

When Mr. Mishkin saw that he had nothing more to hide, and that his inner conflict between the false ideology he had chosen for himself and the shame in admitting his mistake had come to an end, he was able to fulfill his dream of many years. And when he did that, he was surprised by the ease with which his change of heart was accepted.

The neighbors no longer nodded their heads when Reb Shmuel built his sukkah, even though they still wondered. "Let's say that until now you had to build the sukkah for Mr. Mishkin — but why now?"

Actually, Reb Shmuel had also thought that way to begin with. But when he told Mr. Mishkin what he had been thinking, the latter cried out, "You may not know but I wasn't the only one who slipped into your sukkah..." More than that, he refused to say. And Reb Shmuel refrained from asking.

Twenty years have passed since then. Reb Shmuel and Mr. Mishkin both passed from this world at a ripe old age. But if you happen to be passing though that neighbor-hood, where many of the residents are still far from religion, on the day after Yom Kippur, you'll be able to see Reb Shmuel's two sons trying to match up two boards.

No one is puzzled anymore about it, nor by the sign hanging permanently, from holiday to holiday: "Let all who are hungry come and eat."

The Twenty-sixth Menorah

News spread like wildfire throughout the large town. Onchik, who was known as "the *gvir's* servant," had been caught in the middle of the night in the company of the infamous thief Heikin. In their possession were a number of bags filled to the brim with the most expensive, exquisite silver menorahs ever seen. The police, who had secretly followed Heikin's trail from the time he had descended from the mountains (which is where he was wont to hide with the members of his band), saw with their own eyes how Heikin lugged the heavy sacks and gave them to Onchik, Rushing out of their hiding places, they handcuffed the two and began to examine the contents of the bags.

And what do you think they found, if not twenty-six large and costly silver menorahs?

When the policemen asked Onchik why he was trading in stolen goods, especially goods like these, stolen by the chief robber, Heikin, Onchik replied innocently that the menorahs belonged to Yom Tov Rondowitz the *gvir*, that they had been stolen from him a month ago, and that the thief had sent them back by way of a *sheliach mitzvah*, none other than Heikin.

This reply, of course, infuriated the policemen, to whom Heikin was not known for wasting his time on mitzvos but rather the opposite. Onchik's explanation drew only derisive laughter from the crowd which had gathered around them.

"How can the so-called *gvir* purchase even one of these menorahs," they said, "when he doesn't have the money to pay his servant's salary or even buy food?"

Before we continue, there is one thing you should know: Yom Tov Rondowitz was not really a *gvir*, or even half a *gvir*. To understand why he was nonetheless called by the title "*gvir*," we must go back thirty years in time.

Thirty years before Onchik's arrest, Rondowitz had indeed been a very prominent and wealthy *gvir*, owner of vast amounts of cash, land, and property. One day, though, Rondowitz's fortune changed, and he went bankrupt. His property was confiscated by his many creditors, and he became the stingiest of the stingy. Sad to say, he lost not only his money but his mind. No matter which way you looked at it, he was simply insane.

His fellow townsmen soon learned that the *gvir* was mentally affected to such a degree that he had no inkling of his sorry state and continued to believe that he was still the wealthiest and most important man in the entire region.

The truth of the matter was that Yom Tov Rondowitz had nary a crumb of bread with which to revive his soul, and chances were that he would have died of starvation within a few days.

Salvation came in the form of Onchik, a Jewish boy whom he had taken in off the streets several years previously, employing him as a hired servant. Onchik, whose first name was unknown to anyone save himself, continued to serve Rondowitz as if the *gvir* had not lost everything and continued to pay his salary just like in the good days.

Soon enough, the townsmen came to the conclusion that Yom Tov Rondowitz would, before going completely insane, take his servant Onchik with him. That's because not only did Onchik not receive any payment for his services but he even had to use his own money to buy food for the *gvir*, food which continued to be the finest, as he was accustomed to. Worst of all, in everyone's opinion, was the degrading and disgraceful way the *gvir* treated Onchik — like a king would treat a slave, as if the *gvir* were still wealthy.

This fact was substantiated for the townsfolk whenever Onchik took the mad *gvir* for a walk through the town. The *gvir* would shout at his "servant" for all sorts of ridiculous reasons, even raising his cane threateningly at him when he wasn't satisfied. When passersby asked Onchik how he tolerated the *gvir*'s behavior and why he didn't retaliate, he would reply questioningly, "How can I? I am his servant, aren't I?"

These words caused the *gvir*'s creditors to suspect that the *gvir* had a fortune in cash hidden away, so they rushed to his house and searched it thoroughly. When they didn't find what they wanted, they quickly turned upon the one who had caused them to trouble themselves with the search — Onchik. By the time they were finished telling him what they thought of him, Onchik looked crushed.

All this occurred thirty years prior to the fateful day on which Onchik was found in the company of the infamous thief Heikin, twenty-six menorahs worth hundreds of thousands of rubles in his possession. Over those years, the townsmen had nearly forgotten about Onchik, regarding him as a strange man and nothing more. Actually, they didn't even deign to notice him at all.

When he was caught, the townsmen put two and two together and concluded that Onchik was nothing but a secret accomplice of that same robber who lived in the mountains, Heikin, and that over a period of thirty years Onchik had been robbing them, under the guise of being the *gvir*'s servant.

This suspicion flew like feathers in the wind and, in the opinion of most, Onchik deserved to be placed in solitary confinement for the rest of his life, along with his partner, the infamous robber Heikin.

Apparently, though, a minority of the townspeople thought differently. A few dozen people, among them prominent lawyers, important merchants and wealthy landowners, defended Onchik. They volunteered to plead his case in court, visited him in his prison cell to raise his spirits, and used all their connections to try to get him released.

In a matter of days, Onchik was freed from jail, and the surprised townspeople learned that not only had Onchik not been charged with any crime but that the policemen who released him had treated him with the utmost respect, and that none other than the chief of police himself had taken Onchik in his private carriage, laden with the so-called "stolen" menorahs, from jail straight to the house of Yom Tov Rondowitz the *gvir*, who greeted his "servant" with a scowl and lashed out at him for having neglected his duties.

✑ *Chapter Two*

It seems that when the *gvir* lost his clarity of mind and sank into a dream world, all of his numerous servants, workers, and secretaries deserted him and found other positions, forgetting all about their former boss, who had once treated them so kindly.

Only one person remained faithful to him. Only one person remained behind in the large mansion and continued to cater to him as in days gone by: the thin servant with the ascetic appearance — Onchik.

When the food supply in the *gvir's* house began to diminish, Onchik replenished it, purchasing new provisions with his own money. The food, however, that Onchik bought was food that he himself was used to; the *gvir* pushed this food away and shouted at his servant for not paying sufficient attention to his duties. Onchik would then run out and buy finer food, even though he knew that the price of one meal of the type the *gvir* was used to would cost him a quarter of his monthly salary.

Quite rapidly, Onchik's supply of ready cash dwindled, and he had to hire himself out at various and sundry jobs so that he would have enough money to continue supporting his master, the *gvir*.

He accepted only those positions which would not interfere with his primary occupation as the chief servant of the *gvir*. That's how it came to be that the townspeople saw him working as a garbage collector in the early morning, as a porter for a number of hours during the day, and, in the evenings, as a waiter at different wedding. Between jobs, Onchik would rush to the *gvir's* house to serve him, as well as to receive a few shouts and complaints and shakings of the cane for his unsatisfactory service.

Onchik earned quite a nice living from his other jobs
— enough to support his master in style, and even to save a
bit for hard times.

And such a time did come — at the beginning of
Kislev, four years after the *gvir* had gone bankrupt, with
Chanukah only a few weeks away.

On one of those days, the *gvir* turned to his servant
and told him, "I am quite certain it's been several years
since I bought myself a new silver menorah. Surely you
know of my family's tradition of purchasing a new menorah
every year and are aware that I once owned the largest and
most exquisite menorah collection in the country. To my
dismay, though," the *gvir* revealed to his servant, "a number
of years ago the collection was lost, and now I must purchase a new menorah."

Onchik listened in silence. He knew quite well that
the *gvir* had never lost the menorahs but that they had been
taken by the many creditors during the bankruptcy which
was the cause of his master's mental confusion. For obvious
reasons, he did not express his view of the situation to the
gvir.

"The point is, today we are going to buy a new
menorah," the *gvir* announced to his servant.

In a matter of hours, the *gvir* was seen walking down
the main street of the town dressed in his finest outfit,
purchased, of course, by his servant, who supported him so
he would not fall. The two walked quite a distance, until
they stood at the entrance of a small silver shop.

Without hesitation, the *gvir* pointed to the largest
menorah in the window and said to Onchik, "This one."

When they entered the shop, the *gvir* asked the
owner the menorah's price.

"Three thousand rubles," he replied.

Onchik turned pale and tried to bargain with him but the *gvir* silenced him. "Aren't you ashamed? Is it becoming to the *gvir* of Rondowitz for one of his staff to bicker over a few thousand rubles?" At the end of this tirade, the *gvir* instructed the owner of the store to pack up the large menorah, emphasizing that his servant would arrange the matter of payment.

After Onchik helped bring his master home, while apologizing the entire the way for his errant behavior, he rushed to his purse and found two thousand rubles in it. The sum was considered "huge," yet it was not enough to buy the menorah.

At this point, Onchik rushed around trying to get loans to make up the difference but his fellow townsmen would not trust this strange person who dared to ask them for such a large sum as one thousand rubles. Thus, they threw him, shamed and humiliated, out of their homes.

Onchik, though, did not despair. He approached the local banker, Rappaport, for a loan. Rappaport laughed in his face, and told him that he would loan him the money only if he brought him a written guarantee signed by Myerson, the cynical and heartless municipal attorney.

Another person might have regarded this suggestion as an outright rejection of his request. That's exactly what the banker intended. Onchik, however, needed the loan in order to purchase a menorah for the *gvir*, so he headed for Myerson's luxurious office, come what may.

Myerson was taken aback by the beggar who had burst into his office and considered throwing him out, but before he was able to summon one of his assistants, Onchik had already sat down in one of the comfortable chairs and had begun to state his strange request. Myerson discovered that sitting before him was the most unusual person he had ever met.

Myerson gave Onchik quite a lot of his time. He asked him numerous questions on a wide range of subjects, all of which had absolutely nothing to do with Onchik's request for a loan. At a certain point, Myerson invited his entire staff into his office and asked Onchik to repeat his story. Onchik did this in a dry voice, not understanding why such a fuss was being made.

If Onchik had taken a good look around him, he would have noticed a number of esteemed gentlemen in the room wiping their eyes with their handkerchiefs. But Onchik was oblivious to his surroundings, save for noticing one elderly white-haired man, who looked at him strangely.

After he had finished speaking, everyone left the room, and Onchik felt certain that his request had been denied. Soon enough, though, Mr. Myerson returned and gave Onchik a guarantee for a five-hundred-ruble loan.

And what did the white-haired man do if not put an additional five hundred rubles into Onchik's hand?

Onchik looked at them in surprise, hurriedly thanked them, and left quickly, afraid they might change their minds.

Little did he know that long after he left, the lawyers sat in Myerson's deluxe office doing nothing but reflecting deeply on the unique person who had entered their office, their lives and their hearts.

Onchik received the remainder of the money from the stunned banker, who wondered what there was about this shabby man that made him succeed where big businessmen had tried in vain to extract even a recommendation from this cold-hearted lawyer, not to speak of a letter of guarantee officially signed and sealed.

From there, Onchik headed to the silver store and purchased the luxurious menorah the *gvir* so desired.

On the first night of Chanukah, Onchik placed the costly menorah at the entrance to the *gvir*'s home and tenderly filled one of its glass vessels with oil, as if he was about to light it himself. Afterward, the *gvir* stepped outside, recited the blessing in a sweet voice, and kindled the first Chanukah light.

Suddenly, he burst into sobs which shook his whole body. Onchik thought that the unfortunate man had regained a tiny bit of his sanity and had begun, for a moment, to comprehend his difficult situation.

Because Onchik was so involved in watching his master, he did not notice several carriages standing at a distance from the *gvir*'s home. Seated in them were a number of people, such as Myerson the attorney and his staff, and even Rappaport the banker, to whom the entire story had been told and who regarded it as the most touching of the many stories he had heard in his whole life. And he had heard quite a few.

ᔆ Chapter Three

At the end of Chanukah, the *gvir* turned to his servant and said, "Because you have pleased me this time, next year I just might let you use this precious menorah, after I obtain a new one, in line with our long-standing family tradition."

Onchik was delighted that the *gvir* was finally pleased with him. On the other hand, he understood quite well that he had to start putting aside a good amount of money for the following year.

Onchik planned his steps well. He began to work extra hours, dividing his salary into thirds: one-third for day-to-day expenses, a third for repayment of the debt, and a third to be saved for next Chanukah.

At the beginning of Kislev of the following year, Onchik once again took his master to the silver store, and once again the *gvir* pointed to the largest and most expensive menorah in the window. Onchik discovered that the *gvir*'s lack of mental clarity had not impaired his taste in menorahs.

Onchik, too embarrassed to approach Myerson again, was forced to search for a loan. When people refused him, Rappaport the banker rallied to his aid and mentioned that Myerson had, in the past, been Onchik's guarantor.

Upon Rappaport's advice, the various moneylenders asked Myerson about Onchik's credibility, and he in turn, warmly recommended him, telling them the entire story. As a result, his new lenders provided him with not inconsiderable amounts to help him reach his goal.

That year, two menorahs stood on the doorstep of the *gvir*'s mansion, and from a distance, another few carriages whose passengers watched the amazing scene unfolding before their eyes joined the crowd.

Thus the years passed. The *gvir* grew older, and his situation deteriorated. He suffered from delusions of grandeur, believing not only that he was the wealthiest person in the world but also that he ruled over the entire world, or at least a large part of it.

Onchik, for his part, never hinted to his master that things were otherwise, because he knew that such a thought was liable to destroy the *gvir*'s good mood and cast him into a state of profound depression. Onchik had no desire for the *gvir* to become sad, not in any way and no matter what it cost. Especially no matter what it cost.

Between one Chanukah and the next, when Onchik was not busy acquiring menorahs, the *gvir* demanded that he arrange meetings for him with various lawyers and real estate agents. From within his completely imaginary world, he would decide to buy or sell property.

Onchik, who knew quite well that the only property his master owned was the grave he had once bought, remarked that this wasn't the best time to sell land, with the situation so unsettled. Upon hearing this, the *gvir* became angry at Onchik, refusing to speak with him for a number of days. There was nothing worse for Onchik than one of his master's bad moods. That's why he again turned to Myerson, this time asking for his cooperation in a small deception.

Myerson, it turned out, was enthusiastic about the idea and quickly drafted his office staff into the ruse, asking them to issue "documents" regarding various plots of land. Myerson even contacted a number of realtors who eagerly joined the effort as soon as they heard the human-interest story behind it.

When everything was ready, Onchik brought the *gvir* to the offices of Zamenhoff and Goldstein, where the *gvir* proceeded to offer imaginary plots of land for sale. He demanded, naturally, a high price, and the heads of the company were "summoned" to negotiate with him. Suddenly, the *gvir* was transported back to those wonderful years when he had been a prosperous businessman. He argued, stamped his feet, praised his "property" and presented data on profit and loss. The people before him proved to be hard-nosed businessmen, of the type with whom he had always enjoyed working.

At last, he forced them to "compromise," compromised a bit himself, too, and finally, they made a "deal" in which they sold the "property," in exchange for other property — which never was and never would be.

The entire matter was, of course, a farce, and a terrible waste of time for those involved. Nonetheless, they did not let the *gvir* get wind of their feelings.

When the sides finally reached an agreement, lawyers were urgently summoned — Myerson's men — who had been hiding all along in an adjoining room, waiting to be called. The deal was "signed," and both sides made a *l'chayim*.

Throughout the entire meeting, the *gvir* presented Onchik as his servant. He scowled at him and hinted to him that he was about to fire him. Those present, who were fully aware of that faithful servant's devotion, said not a word. However, at the close of the "ceremony," they turned to Onchik and asked him, "Why do you agree to be a slave to that heartless, foolish old man?"

Onchik looked at them in bewilderment. "He didn't take you in off the street twenty years ago. You don't know Yom Tov Rondowitz, the good-hearted and charitable *gvir*. You only know this broken and ailing man. True, he is not that rich and he isn't able to pay my salary but are you certain that's a reason to desert him?

"I love him," declared Onchik, and hastened to take his tired master back home after the long and grueling business deal he had just concluded. He then closed the door, leaving behind a group of confused businessmen, stirred to the depths of their souls by Onchik's devotion, proud of themselves for having been able to offer at least a minimal amount of help to so pure-hearted a man, and, if the truth be told, a little bit envious of the old man who had merited so loyal a servant.

❧ Chapter Four

The years passed. Myerson, the advocate, left this world but his son, who had heard about the remarkable servant from his father, continued to cooperate with Onchik every Kislev, when the *gvir* demanded his yearly menorah.

Twenty-nine years had passed since the *gvir* had gone bankrupt. Twenty-five menorahs crowded his dark warehouse. At last, the thirtieth year was ushered in, and one more menorah joined the collection, the most elaborate and most expensive of them all. It had cost Onchik eight thousand rubles — four thousand from his personal savings, two thousand which he had taken, as usual, on loan, and the remaining two thousand, given to him by those few people in his confidence.

Those were days when the *gvir*'s health declined, long days during which he would sink into a black bitterness.

At times, Onchik would feel that the *gvir*'s sanity was returning. But there were also many days during which the *gvir* did not exchange a single word with Onchik. Sometimes, Yom Tov Rondowitz the *gvir* would sit silently in the guest room, which had once been as elegant as a wedding hall and had bustled with visitors. For hours on end he would sit there without saying a word. Sometimes, his eyes would become watery. But he wasn't crying. He never cried.

Then, one night, thieves broke into the mansion and made a thorough search. They found nothing — except the twenty-six menorahs. When morning came, Onchik discovered that the entire collection was missing.

At that time, there were a lot of break-ins to the town's residents' homes. It was Heikin's notorious band of robbers whose members used to come down from the hills to steal, rob and plunder. These violent bandits cast their terror on the entire town while the police, for their part, were helpless.

Onchik, though, was not fazed by the terrifying stories he had heard about the bandits, and that very day, he packed a bag with a little food and began to climb the mountains in search of the thieves who had stolen the *gvir*'s menorahs.

Onchik knew quite well that if the *gvir* discovered that his collection had been stolen he would, out of deep sorrow, die on the spot. Onchik did not want his beloved *gvir* to die. Nor did he want the *gvir* to be sad.

Therefore, he made the dangerous trek up the hill and, soon enough, found himself facing the barrels of a dozen loaded pistols, held by the same number of bandits.

They took him to their cave, where they questioned him thoroughly.

Onchik explained to them in his usual dry tone that he had come to look for the menorahs stolen from his master, especially menorah number 26, which the *gvir* needed for lighting the Chanukah lights.

Naturally, these words made the bandits laugh, for never before in their lives had they heard of a man willing to take the risk of climbing those mountains carrying only a lunch bag — and that, in order to retrieve a menorah which did not even belong to him.

After they had finished mocking him, they made plans to kill him. However, one member of the gang suggested that their leader, none other than Heikin himself, deserved a good laugh too, for laughter is a rare commodity in the lives of those living in the mountains.

Bound and handcuffed, Onchik was brought to their leader's den. The gang sat him down and presented to their leader the strange man they had met. Onchik was not impressed by the character sitting opposite him and hastened to further the matter for which he had come.

"Are you the chief robber, Heikin?" asked Onchik. "If so, I have a deal to offer you. I am willing to forgo all of the other menorahs which belong to the *gvir* on the condition that you give me the twenty-sixth menorah, the one I urgently need. Actually, I am willing to accept it on loan from you or even to rent it and return it immediately after Chanukah."

Roars of laughter were heard throughout the robbers' den. They were abruptly silenced, though, by a wave of the hand of their leader, Heikin, who did not laugh at all.

"Tell me," he said in a soft voice. "What is your relationship to that *gvir*.

Onchik sat and told. In a dry, factual tone, he presented to Heikin and his fellow robbers the story of the twenty-sixth menorah and the problem facing him in purchasing another menorah when his credit had run out. When Onchik finished speaking, he wondered, aloud, from where the dust had come which had entered the robbers' eyes, causing tears. Onchik's own eyes were absolutely dry, and he reasoned that the dust probably hadn't been able to reach them because his back was to the opening of the cave.

For a long time the robbers remained silent and stared at the thin and tortured figure of Onchik. One of them expressed his opinion that Onchik deserved an honorary medal of courage. But Onchik told him that he wouldn't know what to do with such a toy and declared that he would be satisfied with the menorah.

After a few long moments, during which Heikin was immersed in thought, he turned to Onchik and said, "Return to your home, good man. Return to the home of your master, loyal and brave servant. Within two days, all of the menorahs will be returned to you, for it is not my band which has stolen them, and it will take a few days until I get them for full cost from one of the other bands swarming in this area."

Heikin even provided Onchik with a bodyguard, who accompanied him back to town, and within the day, Onchik had safely returned to his master's home.

Exactly two days later, Heikin came down from the mountain burdened with sacks, and it was then that the arrest, which we described at the beginning of this story, took place.

Soon, though, Onchik was released from jail, thanks to the help of the lawyers and important merchants, who knew quite well the story of the twenty-six menorahs. It seems that Heikin the thief had revealed the full story to his interrogators, and that the very same dust which had flown into his eyes in his robbers' den in the mountains when Onchik had told his story, had made its way into the eyes of the policemen.

Rapidly, the entire story spread within the town — and without it as well. It was one of the most remarkable, and one of the saddest, stories ever told — a chronicle of devotion, self-sacrifice, good character traits, a good heart, gratitude, and loyalty.

To the surprise of all, Heikin the notorious robber announced his resignation from his business of thievery. "I turned to this path," he said, "because I saw a corrupt and evil world, filled with people who were willing to sacrifice others to achieve their own aims. I despaired of that world, and so I went on to this errant way — until I met this unfortunate servant. Only then did I see a ray of light in the world.

"Imagine how the world would look if there were a few more pure-hearted people like Onchik," said Heikin. "Would there be room for theft and corruption in such a world? Would anyone dare commit the deeds I used to?"

❧ Chapter Five

It was the first night of Chanukah. All the townspeople assembled opposite the old mansion of Yom Tov Rondowitz the *gvir*. When the designated time arrived, the loyal servant Onchik stepped outside, wheeling the chair on which the *gvir* was seated.

The *gvir* was ninety years old; his strength had waned. However, on hearing the commotion around him, he lifted his head and saw the hundreds of people who had gathered around to see him. He did not suspect that it was actually his servant they had come to see. Suddenly, a new spirit began to stir within him. He took his candle and in a loud voice pronounced the three blessings, a smile of contentment covering his face as he heard the thunderous "amen."

Then his face paled. A hush descended on the crowd. All bent their ears to hear what he had to say.

"Come here, my beloved servant," the *gvir*'s voice was heard.

Onchik, who had never before heard such words from his master's mouth, moved closer, bewildered, to the *gvir*.

"Sit down beside me, Mordechai Onchik, chief servant of the House of Rondowitz," the *gvir* commanded.

Onchik bent over slightly, and the old man placed a hand on his head.

"I hereby bequeath to you my entire mansion and all of my property, including my costly menorah collection," proclaimed the *gvir*, and here he added in a trembling and somewhat hesitant voice, "I also bequeath to you my title. Rise, stand on your feet, the future *gvir* of the House of Rondowitz."

The startled Onchik rose. The *gvir* struggled to pull himself up, barely managing to stand, and kissed Onchik on the forehead.

The entire throng burst into tears at the sight, the likes of which none of them had ever seen.

An expression of satisfaction covered Onchik's face. This was the first time he had seen his master genuinely and thoroughly pleased.

✌ The End

Onchik continued to serve his master with endless love and devotion for several months, until the *gvir* closed his eyes forever. From that time on, Onchik was called *gvir* by all, with not a single person adding even the slightest smile at the title. Chances are that Onchik was the only porter and garbage man since the creation of the world to bear the title "*gvir*."

For many years, the townspeople would bring their children to gaze at Onchik, hoping that they would absorb at least a little of his good traits. Onchik would smile at them but could never understand what all the fuss was about.

Over the years, Onchik sold the menorah collection he owned, except for the twenty-sixth menorah, which he reserved for his own use.

The *gvir*, Mordechai Onchik, became a prominent and dignified personage whose his acts of kindness gained wide acclaim. Until his death at a ripe old age the townspeople attended the ceremony of the kindling of the first Chanukah light at his mansion, which each time reminded them anew of the exalted levels to which human good-heartedness and character can reach — and how great is the power of loyalty and devotion.

From All My Teachers

It was early in the morning, the culmination of a long night — Shavuos night.

Many of the members of the Sha'arei Zion shul looked on in amazement at the rare scene which unfolded before their eyes. The stern, elderly Reb Shulem Ruzhin, often called a *Yekke* because of his origin and character, was conversing with a fifteen-year-old boy, and had not only closed his Gemara for that purpose, but had even allowed himself to laugh with the boy.

Reb Shulem's fellow worshipers, long accustomed to seeing him bent over his Gemara the entire Shavuos night, oblivious to his surroundings, had never in their lives witnessed such a scene. Reb Shulem wasn't a particularly gregarious person, and it was rare to see a smile cross his lips. The strange combination of Reb Shulem pausing from his studies and laughing with a fifteen-year-old boy who could have been his grandson, heightened the already whetted curiosity of the onlookers.

One of the few young people who had remained in the shul the entire night told the older congregants, who had arrived in time for *shacharis*, that at about midnight the boy had arrived with his father, a well-known *avrech*, and that the two had spoken at length with Reb Shulem, until at a certain point, the father had left while the boy remained behind, deep in conversation with Reb Shulem.

Had you, the reader, taken a peek at the boy, you wouldn't have believed your eyes — even though you are still not familiar with the characters of the story — because the boy didn't look at all like the child of a *charedi* family, especially not one headed by a well-known *avrech*. But from the boy's determined expression it was apparent to all that he was "one of those cases," and all heads nodded in sympathy for the famous and distinguished rabbi whose lot it was to have in his charge the boy found under the huge mop of hair topped by a tiny yarmulke.

A few hours before — quite close to midnight — Reb Eliyahu, the youth's father, had sat in the Divrei Moshe shul watching his son wander around the benches of those sitting and learning, and his heart had broken.

The boy was obviously in his teens. He was relatively tall for his age, and his face looked older than his years. His features, which until a year and a half ago had been as delicate as a child's, had suddenly changed, yet still hadn't assumed their final form. Reb Eliyahu knew that the same was true about the boy's personality. He sensed that his son was in a state of transition, whose end result no one knew. In the meantime, Reb Eliyahu could only go by rumors and by what he himself perceived. The picture was far from encouraging.

He looked at his son, who went from bench to bench, making jokes — probably about himself, in his latest self-styled defensive manner — ignoring the occasional hints of those studying who tried to brush him off with "*veiter,*

veiter." He watched him try to prolong the conversation as much as possible, until he spotted another pair whom it looked like he could engage in idle conversation. He then cut short his conversation with the first pair as suddenly as he had begun. Reb Eliyahu watched him as he approached the next pair of study partners, saw him put a friendly hand on the shoulder of one, and say, "I hear you have a question in learning?" Reb Eliyahu heard their laughter. Asher, who had spent the night wandering in and out of the tea room was going to solve a complex question on the Gemara! Why, there's no better joke!

Reb Eliyahu might have laughed at Asher's joke himself — except that when it came to Asher, no joke seemed funny to him... for he was his son.

Yes, this was Asher, his beloved son, the most brilliant of them all, the son from whom he had expected so much, the son who even as a young child had given him so much *nachas*, who was the smartest one in his class, whose abilities and sharp mind, especially his sharp mind, had been acclaimed by all. This was Asher, with whom he had studied several hours every Shabbos, until his other sons complained that he favored him over them. And he had to admit that he did. He really enjoyed studying with his son and relished the thought that if Asher displayed such unusual talent at such a young age, there was no doubt as to what the future would hold.

Never in a million years had there been the slightest doubt that this son would develop into a real scholar, a true *lamdan*. More than that, he had believed that his son had a serious, mature character. Even at a young age it was obvious that the child had a well-developed independence of thought. His saw his son's seriousness, his unbounded curiosity, and his ability to comprehend subtleties that even those older than he didn't even suspect existed.

But above all, Reb Eliyahu was familiar with his son's outlook on life and the views he held — views which led him to believe that the child would become a true leader. The boy was able to distinguish between proper and improper behavior, between genuine piety and sham. Reb Eliyahu delighted in his son's deep understanding, on his proper attitude, and on the *yiras shamayim* manifest in his views. Sometimes, Asher would fall into speaking negatively about certain people, and he, Reb Eliyahu, would rebuke him. Actually, these rebukes weren't that sharp, since Reb Eliyahu himself felt exactly the same way, and when his son would point this out to him, Reb Eliyahu used to reply, "First of all, not every thought should be expressed, and besides, there's a big difference in our ages, don't you agree?"

Reb Eliyahu began to recall his past efforts to instill his son with *yiras shamayim* and correct *hashkafah*. Mostly, he had directed his efforts towards training the child to think properly. Aware of Asher's brain power, he had always felt it best to focus on the child's intellect rather than on his emotions. "The moment this child thinks, he also feels, and not the opposite," he would tell his wife. "As soon as I implant a certain thought in his mind, it becomes an integral part of him."

He recalled how he had explained the logic behind mitzvah observance, and how meticulous and stringent they had always been in their home when it came to kashrus. It reached the point that whenever there was a celebration in the *cheder* — in honor of a *siyum*, a holiday, or even the birthday of a fellow classmate — it went without saying that it was Asher's mother who baked the cake. Everyone knew why. It was supposed to be a secret known only by the principal and Asher's teachers but in a way no one could explain, probably having something to do with Asher's quick mind, the reason was divulged to all: Asher's parents didn't want their son to eat foods with a *hechsher* they didn't use in their own home. Not that they cast aspersions, G-d forbid, on the validity of other kitchens. It was just their strong desire to be exacting about kashrus, to the point where they didn't want even to take the slightest risk that their children would, *chas v'chalilah*, stumble and eat something that wasn't of the highest standard.

Reb Eliyahu remembered how proud he had been of his wife's dedication. He knew, too, that the principal also regarded it highly, and this knowledge did nothing to diminish his good feelings.

But now, the thought of the chocolate bar without a top-quality *hechsher*, which he had found only a week ago in Asher's drawer, plummeted him back to painful reality with a thud. How had something like that happened?

Even worse, Reb Eliyahu knew quite well that the chocolate bar, like other aspects of Asher's behavior he had become aware of, was only an outward manifestation of a problem far more serious. His son Asher was losing his faith. His son Asher still went with a *kippah* and tzitzis but he treated all things holy with indifference. His son Asher made light of prayers, blessings and mitzvos.

From the moment the Evil Inclination had taken up residence in his son's heart, not a day passed without its conquering more territory. And so, Asher's degeneration progressed from day to day.

If, when Asher first entered yeshivah, the *mashgiach* had been full of praise for Asher's scholastic abilities and sharp mind, a few months later he passed right by Reb Eliyahu with nothing more than a curt hello. Reb Eliyahu was perplexed. He tried to push it to the back of his mind, afraid of what he would hear. Soon enough, though, the *mashgiach* asked to speak with him. At first, the complaints were about coming in late to prayers and problems with the other boys; later, complaints were heard about the "rebellious attitude he exudes in the yeshivah." His studies were still unchanged.

It was understood, of course, that Reb Eliyahu talked with his son about it. Asher, though, explained to his father his criticisms of the yeshivah's administration, and his criticisms sounded justified. Asher was critical of the quality of the instructor and of the fact that he couldn't manage to control the class. Asher presented his father with a picture of a teacher who talked about all sorts of things, like the social problems of the students, instead of learning. He said that by talking about those childish problems, he was lowering the standard of the class. "It's like on a fifth-grade level, not like in *yeshivah ketanah*," Asher explained to his father.

Reb Eliyahu listened to his son's explanation and told him that it wasn't his job to criticize the instructors. His protest was weak, and the weakness made a deep impression on Asher.

In ensuing discussions with the *mashgiach*, it became clear that while there were a lot of peer problems in Asher's class, Asher was the one responsible for the disturbances. "He has a slyness not found in boys his age," the *mashgiach* said. "He can convince anyone of anything. He manipulates everyone — myself included — to go along with his craziness. There are boys who follow his instructions, while he remains in the shadows. Listen, Reb Eliyahu, this is one of those cases where I would advise you not to remain complacent. I would suggest you stop admiring the boy so much and instead make it clear to him what it means to be a *naval bi'reshus haTorah* — a person who, even though he may not transgress explicit prohibitions, manages to circumvent the spirit of the Torah to get what he wants."

From then on, Reb Eliyahu refused to speak with the *mashgiach*. Not only that, but during the following days he continued to criticize nonstop "that same *avrech* who thinks he knows something about education." Over and over again he told his wife, his married children, his sons-in-law, and even his friends on the yeshivah's staff, about the *mashgiach* who had called his son a *naval bi'reshus ha-Torah*. "Whoever uses such expressions to describe a student is unworthy of being a *mashgiach!*" cried Reb Eliyahu, who did not trouble himself to quote the *mashgiach* accurately and tell his listeners that the *mashgiach* had only recommended explaining the meaning of the concept "*naval bi'reshus haTorah*" to Asher. Reb Eliyahu also did not take the trouble to watch his speech, and, sure enough, his remarks reached the sensitive ears of Asher.

From then on, there was a rapid decline. The situation in the yeshivah worsened. The administration finally decided to send Asher home. Reb Eliyahu left no stone unturned to prove to whomever necessary that the yeshivah's administration had no idea how to treat the students, and the proof was right there: they were making a scapegoat out of his son, whose excellence required no proof, and were kicking him out.

As a result of Reb Eliyahu's pressures, Asher was permitted to return to the yeshivah under very strict conditions. Asher complained that these conditions lowered his prestige in the yeshivah, and his father tried to encourage him, explaining that life is full of challenges and that it was enough that he, his father, knew that he was right and thought highly of him.

But the boy complained that he had lost his desire to learn, and to the list of complaints about Asher's social problems was now added a complaint about a big drop in his studies, to the extent that he was wasting time and causing the other boys in the class to waste time, too. Gradually Reb Eliyahu learned about the unsuitable friends Asher had collected both within the yeshivah and without, and about Asher's overall spiritual degeneration — and he felt his entire world crumbling around him.

He then began to run to *gedolei* Torah and influential community leaders, crying to them that "they've stolen my child." He presented them with evidence of Asher's excellent academic record in the Talmud Torah. He wept bitterly — real, heartfelt tears — over his high hopes, which were being rapidly dashed, for his beloved child who was being pushed into the abyss, according to him, by people lacking experience. He was willing to do anything, yes, anything, in order to have things go back to the way they were — but the matter, it seemed, was out of his hands.

As if that weren't enough, Reb Eliyahu himself began to discern signs of his son's degeneration — in the snatches of conversations he overheard, in the friends Asher brought home, in the lack of his usual enthusiasm. How had his serious, intelligent son turned into a shallow, irresponsible teenager?

Reb Eliyahu scolded Asher for his behavior. And when matters reached the point where his behavior wasn't suitable for a boy from a *charedi* family, his father exploded. Asher, in turn, shed his normal filial respect and answered him back, using coarse language which left Reb Eliyahu startled and pale, wondering where Asher had learned to act that way. He lost his self-control and vented all the pent-up emotions of past months on his son, turning to his other children, young and old alike, and shouting, "Stay away from him! I don't want him to ruin you, too!"

From that point on, the relationship between Asher and his father changed drastically. They did not speak to each other, except for the well-aimed barbs which Reb Eliyahu made about his son's character. If at first Reb Eliyahu's cynical remarks had caused Asher to shrink in pain, he rapidly adopted a strange line of defense: Instead of trying to refute his father's charges, he agreed with them pleasantly, even adding self-denigrating comments here and there. Asher thus managed to create an image of himself in the family's eye as a rebel who simply didn't care what others said about him.

Sometimes, though, he would burst out in pain, and anyone with even the most minimal understanding of the human soul would have realized that these outbursts came from a wounded heart. But in Asher's family, no one understood the human soul; they only saw behavior. And Asher's behavior was growing worse from day to day.

They found out about his difficult spiritual state from his new friends, some of whom even came from "good families," others, from broken homes. Reb Eliyahu would shame Asher for associating with such friends, ripping him apart with cutting remarks like, "Birds of a feather flock together," and, "Tell me who your friends are, and I'll tell you who you are!"

Asher would then respond with a sharp retort of his own. And suddenly Reb Eliyahu discovered another side to the sharpness he had cultivated and had so enjoyed — when the sharpness was turned against him. At first, Reb Eliyahu tried to contend with his son verbally, until he realized that it was beneath his dignity to bicker with him. From then on, a cold, impervious curtain separated the two. Although the father's face, like the son's, expressed indifference, in their innermost beings both were deeply pained. Occasionally, Reb Eliyahu would burst out angrily, and for some reason it seemed to him that his son, in his own way, enjoyed those scenes.

"You're acting fresh! You'll be the death of me," he would warn Asher, who would only behave even more brazenly in response.

Because of his behavior and unsuitable companions, Asher was expelled from the yeshivah, and Reb Eliyahu wore himself out, humiliating himself, pleading for his son to be accepted into another yeshivah. Reb Eliyahu would tell everyone about Asher's "guardians" — read "teachers" — who had betrayed their responsibility. When he said this, tears would stream from his eyes, and in the face of his pain and sincere words, a yeshivah which agreed to accept Asher would be found.

But Asher did not change. The transfers from yeshivah to yeshivah only hurt him and lowered him still further, so that after a number attempts, Reb Eliyahu again found himself standing at the sidelines, watching his son's decline. Reb Eliyahu knew all too well the path Asher was treading, was bitterly aware of what lay at the end of that road, and only wondered how it had all begun. He did have an obvious answer, though, one he voiced at every opportunity: the faulty approach of the yeshivah's teachers. Yet deep down a voice whispered to him that even if that were true, their mistake had only been in reaction to his son's behavior, because the fact was that hundreds of other students without exception graduated from that very same yeshivah. The question Reb Eliyahu asked himself was why *his* son? Why he, who was raised since childhood to meticulous mitzvah observance and *yiras shamayim*? Why he out of all of them?

When did all this begin? Reb Eliyahu asked himself. When had the first signs become evident? Perhaps herein would lie the key to the mystery.

From the corner of his eye, Reb Eliyahu saw his son stretched out on a bench, his feet wantonly resting on a chair — and his heart twisted in pain. He buried his head in his hands and tried to hide the scene from his eyes.

With his head still in his hands, Reb Eliyahu recalled a certain incident which had taken place a while back. Every time it came to mind, he would push it to a far corner of his mind. The incident disturbed him from the moment he had heard the first complaint against his son. Yet, for some reason, he had never taken the time to analyze it, to consider the possibility that it was justified. That was, because it involved a person whom Reb Eliyahu did not particularly, or, to be precise, did not at all, esteem. Just a "*ba'al habayis*," Reb Eliyahu would tell himself, a plain old man who had delivered a lecture to him on Asher's future and on the distorted way Reb Eliyahu was raising the boy.

Subconsciously, Reb Eliyahu sensed that the incident threatened him in some way. He knew that if he took it seriously, he, and no one else, would become the one to blame for the evil path his son was taking.

Reb Eliyahu found it hard to reign in his thoughts, and they broke through and raced out of his control.

५~ Part Two

It had happened three years before, when Asher was twelve years old. Asher had been a brilliant, outstanding student, whom all had praised, all accept one — Shulem Ruzhin.

Reb Ruzhin was a well-liked, elderly teacher in the *cheder*, an experienced teacher who had actually stopped teaching many years prior to that incident, except for the one hour a day during which he taught general studies, a remnant of days gone by.

Despite his advanced age and geniality, Reb Shulem controlled the classes he taught with an iron hand. No one knew why but the fact was that most of students both loved him *and* stood in awe of him at the same time.

Most of them but not all. Every year there would be one or two students who would grumble against him, whether openly or secretly.

The reason for this was Reb Shulem's custom of trying to correct the character flaws of those students who he felt required such correction. Reb Shulem wasn't impressed by high grades or by a student's status among his peers. He carefully scrutinized the behavior of each one of his students and, when necessary, would point out where he felt improvements could be made. When the student in question happened to be top ranking, or particularly popular — one of those whose faults teachers sometimes prefer to overlook because of their achievements — Reb Shulem would find that he had acquired a sharp opponent within his classroom.

From the beginning of the year when Asher was in Reb Shulem's class, the latter made sure to reprove him every time he jumped up to answer instead of another boy who found it hard to do so. He would reprove him again and again for behavior that was rooted in arrogance, a trait which, in Reb Shulem's opinion, Asher possessed in abundance.

This was the first time in Asher's life that he had encountered a teacher who didn't commend, praise and extol him in class — rather, the opposite.

And Asher was hurt, very hurt.

But he didn't say a thing to his father. He waited for an opportune time... and that time arrived.

One afternoon after lunch, when it was time to return to class, Asher complained of a "headache" and stayed home for an hour.

The next day, at precisely the same time, Asher again managed to avoid returning to school.

On the third day, his mother sensed something amiss in her son's behavior and questioned him about it.

Asher did not answer.

That evening, when his father came home, he tried to get it out of him. It was clear to him that Asher was hiding something. After much cajoling, Asher finally agreed to say only one thing: "I don't want Reb Shulem for my teacher."

"Why not?"

"I have a reason."

Only after a lot of parental pressure did Asher agree to reveal that his teacher, Reb Shulem, used street language: "Like for instance. . ."

Asher was silent.

His parents tried to get him to say the expressions his teacher had used but Asher remained silent. Only after a great deal of persuasion did he relent and say quietly, "Lately he's been telling a 'daily joke.' Every day he tells a joke which lowers the level of the class, like. . ." Asher repeated one of the teacher's jokes, doing an exact imitation. It was a joke about two New York policemen who stopped a suspicious-looking man (and here the teacher had cast a slur on a certain ethnic group) who was driving a very fancy car. The policemen forced him out of the car, drew a circle on the road, and warned him not to step out of it. While they were busy taking his car apart, the man laughed hysterically. When they finished, one policeman asked the man who was shaking with laughter, "What's so funny?" to which he replied, "When you weren't looking, I went out of the circle three times!"

Even though Asher's parents understood the joke, they didn't laugh at all. In their opinion, the joke shouldn't have been told in a class, and certainly not by a rebbe. As if to confirm their thoughts, Asher declared, "I can't learn with a teacher like that."

Reb Eliyahu and his wife did not reply. On the one hand, they were relieved, and even amazed, by the remarkable piety and sensitivity of their son. On the other hand, they knew that they had to solve the problem.

They went to their room to discuss the issue. A difficult dilemma faced them. While the matter wasn't that serious, they still had, *baruch Hashem*, a sensitive, pious child who had imbibed the special sanctity and purity which prevailed in his home. Would it be right of them to ignore the child's request? From an educational standpoint, could they overlook the pleas of a pure-hearted child who didn't want to hear jokes or expressions which, though not terrible, were still far from refined? "How will we be able to train him to be G-d fearing and sensitive if we ignore a request like this?" Reb Eliyahu's wife wanted to know.

"Perhaps we should discuss the matter with the teacher," Reb Eliyahu suggested.

They waited until their son left for *cheder* and, at the end of Reb Shulem's class, called the school's office.

Reb Shulem was summoned to the telephone and quietly listened to the complaints of Asher's parents. When they had finished speaking, he said, "Do you think it is because of the jokes that he doesn't want to come?"

"What other reason could there be?" asked Reb Eliyahu.

"You have a very clever son," Reb Shulem said. "Perhaps the cleverest student I have ever had, and I've had thousands. There is just something in his *neshamah* which" — Reb Shulem hesitated slightly — "needs a bit of correction?"

Reb Eliyahu felt his blood begin to boil. "My son complains that you tell unacceptable jokes in class and you say his soul requires correction?!"

Reb Shulem remained calm. "Excuse me but my question remains. Do you think he doesn't want to come to class because of the jokes?"

"You're wasting my time. I see that I'm not getting through to you. You'll hear from me yet!" cried Reb Eliyahu as he slammed down the receiver.

Two days passed before Reb Eliyahu and his wife found time to meet with the principal. In the meantime, they told Asher to stay home. Once in the principal's office, they told him the entire story. Further questioning on their part had revealed a few more of Reb Shulem's expressions. They summed up by saying, "You know our son and are aware of his refinement. We have the right to demand that a teacher like that not teach our son."

To their surprise, the principal refused to accept their accusations. "Even though I, too, do not approve of jokes of that type being told in class, and I intend to mention this to Reb Shulem, there is absolutely no connection between that and the terrible step you took in keeping your son home in protest against the teacher. You've committed an educational blunder of the worst degree! Reb Shulem is an experienced teacher and an exceptionally good one, too. He is a tremendous expert on understanding the inner being of a child. If he determined that there is a hidden reason for your son's complaint, then there must be such a reason.

"And if you ask me," added the principal, "I know precisely to what Reb Shulem is referring. Your son is not as refined as you're trying to make him out to be. He is a boy who tries to dominate his class and succeeds in doing so, often at the expense of weaker students. He does it cleverly, sometimes managing to get an entire class not to speak to one of the students. By the way, he always uses methods which are "spiritual," so to speak. He can force the class to ostracize a boy who spoke in the middle of *davening*, or make life miserable for a boy whose father works and who, in Asher's opinion, doesn't learn enough Torah. He mocks the social status, and even the origins, of other students in the class. The only teacher to notice this was Reb Shulem, and since the beginning of the year he has been trying to help Asher improve his character, or at least to lessen the damage he causes in class. Asher has been trying for quite some time to lower Reb Shulem's prestige in the students' eyes. He failed. Now he is attempting to harm Reb Shulem through you, in the same way that he pits his classmates against each other. Do you think that I will allow this to take place?"

Reb Eliyahu and his wife were stunned. They knew their son so well! They saw how careful he was with mitzvah observance, his *yiras shamayim*. True, at home he was also critical — of his brothers and sisters and even of his parents — where spiritual matters were concerned. But all that came from the fire which burned within him. Asher was destined for greatness, and the man seated opposite them who called himself a principal, yet who obviously hadn't the slightest understanding of education, thought that he could teach him, Reb Eliyahu, how to raise his son?

Reb Eliyahu could no longer contain himself. "With all due respect," he exploded, "Reb Shulem is a '*schreiber*,' a general studies teacher, and I have a right to demand that he not try to be a *mechanech*. His responsibility is limited to teaching my son two times two, not to point out his faults. If my son needs his character improved, that's the job of his teacher, not of a simple '*schreiber*.' "

The words had no sooner left Reb Eliyahu's mouth when the principal rose from his seat and said quietly but firmly, "I listened to you, and now it is your turn to listen to me. Your son will remain at home for three days as a punishment for the chutzpah he displayed in not coming to Reb Shulem's class. At the end of that period, you will have to apologize to Reb Shulem, and, if he so permits, Asher will be allowed to return to the *cheder*."

Reb Eliyahu and his wife left the principal's office pale and angry as could be. But Reb Eliyahu was not one to give up. He was not about to let a principal who knew absolutely nothing about education destroy his son. It wasn't a question of his own honor but that the education of his son — a boy whose only sin was having a sensitive soul — was being destroyed.

Reb Eliyahu tired to involve the local rabbi, as well as various people in the *cheder*'s administration in the affair, and even managed to get some of them to side with him,

234 OF THE SOUL

especially when he described the expressions Reb Shulem had dared use in class. However, most of them excused themselves, saying that they could not interfere with the principal's decisions.

In the meantime, the three days passed. During that period, Reb Eliyahu and his wife encouraged their son, even telling him stories about *gedolei Yisrael* who had suffered bitterly because they had stuck to their principles in the face of those more powerful than they. At the end of three days, Reb Eliyahu called Reb Shulem at home and, in a formal tone, expressed his apology for the trouble caused him, while at the same time emphasized that he had been forced to apologize and that he was doing it for his son's sake.

Reb Shulem stopped him in the middle of this forced apology. "If you don't feel it necessary to apologize, I'll excuse you from it. I only ask that you listen to what I wish to say."

Reb Eliyahu waited impatiently to hear what Reb Shulem had to say.

"I understand you," Reb Shulem began. "You listen to your son, and his words are pleasing to your ears. Which father wouldn't be delighted by a son who displays such exceptional *'frumkeit'* while the person who has criticized him is merely a simple *'schreiber'* who teaches two times two.

"However, I am teaching him in the same way that I have taught thousands of children over half a century, and I am telling you that your son's criticism does not come from the good side of his heart but from the bad.

"Asher sees and hears a great deal of criticism in his home against the whole world. He has grown accustomed to deriding other people and to thinking very highly of himself, whether this is warranted or not. These things strengthen the negative part of a person's heart.

"Right now, he is using this part for things which seem to you reasonable and just but his true purposes are completely different. If you aren't smart enough to stop him now," warned Reb Shulem, "the day will come when this negative part will burst out, as it tends to do — but against you! Listen to what a simple '*schreiber*' who understands just a bit about a child's soul has to say."

At that point, Reb Eliyahu cut Reb Shulem short and in a cold voice declared, "Thank you very much for your advice and I hope my son won't hear any more jokes in your class."

Yes, with such blunt words Reb Eliyahu had ended the conversation, with his son listening in from beginning to end, understanding quite well with whom his father sided.

Reb Eliyahu awoke from his reveries with a start. Only now, three years after that conversation, was he ready to admit that Reb Shulem, the simple "*schreiber*," had been right. He started to think back, to review his son's behavior over the past years, only to discover that Asher had always had a problem with his *middos* and that he had developed precisely as Reb Shulem had predicted. Now, as he looked at Asher, Reb Eliyahu realized that Reb Shulem's warnings had materialized in full. He was keenly aware of the wall which had formed between him and his son, of the rift between them, of his son's clever, cynical way of reacting to his father's criticism, and he realized that the way Asher had behaved towards Reb Shulem was the way he was now acting towards his father. How had the predictions of this simple "*schreiber*" come true? How?

Feelings of guilt overcame Reb Eliyahu. He had known all along that Reb Shulem was right. But his pride hadn't let him listen to the words of a simple "*schreiber*." Feelings of remorse crushed his heart, threatening to break it. Making a split-second decision, he rose and went over to his son. "Come with me."

Asher was astonished. His father hadn't said a word to him in months, except for the few caustic and biting remarks he had made about Asher's friends. Asher wondered what his father wanted. "Where are we going?" Asher asked.

"Do you know where your teacher Reb Shulem Ruzhin lives?"

Asher appeared surprised. "What's going on?"

"I want to speak with him!"

Asher told him the address, and his father asked him to come with him.

❧ *Part Three*

It was midnight. The two walked silently through the quiet, empty streets. Reb Eliyahu assumed that Reb Shulem would be studying in a shul near his home. They looked in several, finding him at last in a small *beis midrash* on a side street. As soon as they entered, they saw the figure of Reb Shulem, who had stopped teaching because of his advanced age, bent over a Gemara, his eyes half-closed.

Reb Eliyahu motioned to Asher to follow him, and Asher obeyed.

They sat down opposite him. Reb Shulem was surprised to see his former student and concluded that the man with him must be his father.

"*Gut Yom Tov,*" said Reb Shulem.

"*Gut Yom Tov,*" Reb Eliyahu replied. "I came especially from our neighborhood to apologize to you."

Reb Shulem appeared surprised. "For what?"

"You surely understand why."

"I have a good idea of what you are referring to but it seems to me that you have already apologized."

"Woe to such an apology. Now I would like to apologize from the depths of my heart."

Reb Shulem fell silent. He glanced at the father, and then focused his gaze on the face of the son, on his *blorit*, the shaggy tuft of hair so untypical for a member of his family, and let out a long yes. He understood.

"We were blind," Reb Eliyahu said. "We were deaf. How could we have been so blind? How could our eyes not have seen?" Tears welled up in Reb Eliyahu's eyes, and even the surprised Asher turned aside.

"Is the break, then, so deep?" Reb Shulem asked gently.

"It is worse than you can imagine. Much worse."

"But he still has a yarmulke on his head," Reb Shulem commented.

"But what's hidden under it?" Reb Eliyahu replied. "My son Asher is gradually losing his *emunah*. We see him degenerating before our very eyes and are helpless to do anything about it. My son Asher, my beloved son whom I so admired, in whom I placed so much hope, is distancing himself from me, the source which nurtured him. Yes, he still wears a kippah and even a hat and suit but I know what's in his heart, and I'm aware of what he's doing."

Reb Eliyahu was weeping, while his son, the sensitive boy, buried his head in his hands.

"My son is at the top, or perhaps even halfway down, a steep slope," continued Reb Eliyahu. "I know what lies at the bottom of that slope yet can do nothing to stop him. I have gone to all the *gedolim* and *rabbanim* but their blessings and prayers have remained unanswered. I decided to come to you because the words you said three years ago still echo in my ears. Perhaps you, who even then understood the boy's soul, will know how to repair it. Please forgive me for what I said against you at that time. Now I stand before you like a pauper at the threshold. Perhaps you will know how to bring my beloved son, who is part of my soul, back to me. My methods have failed. He doesn't listen to my criticisms and laughs at me. My beloved, sensitive son, whose *yiras shamayim* was so strong, is going to ruin.

It doesn't even matter to him that my heart is broken. What will become of me? What will become of him?"

Reb Shulem did not reply. He merely gazed at the father and son sitting next to each other, neither looking at the other, their faces reflecting all the sorrow in the world.

Reb Shulem understood. He saw the father's suffering and realized that he was unaware of the tremendous pain his words had caused Asher. Reb Shulem knew that Asher did care, that he cared about his father's broken heart, but that his own heart was also broken.

"I forgive you completely," Reb Shulem said.

"Forgiveness isn't enough for me. I know that your hands hold the key to the mystery's solution. Please, tell me how all this happened, how a child who was a *tzaddik* and a *lamdan*, who was extolled by all, turned into a boy so difficult and crue—" Reb Eliyahu didn't want to utter that word. "How can he be so hard-hearted, so brazen? How can he turn a deaf ear to all my requests and pleas? How —?"

Reb Shulem stopped Reb Eliyahu's harsh words because he saw Asher's expression becoming again closed into the impenetrable mask he had worn when he arrived.

"Please tell me what you saw that I failed to see. If I erred, as apparently I did, tell me so in front of my son. He doesn't respect me anyway. I have nothing to hide from him."

Reb Shulem was momentarily silent, and then began to speak. "Listen, your son Asher is very clever. He is a sharp-witted, talented boy. This boy grew up in a home where all of the mitzvos are meticulously observed and where pointed criticism is heaped on anyone who does not behave similarly.

"Asher absorbed both these attitudes: the strict regard for mitzvah observance, as well as the critical eye. If my guess is correct, at your Shabbos table you speak *divrei Torah* right alongside criticism of people whose behavior does not meet with your approval. The criticism is sharp and cynical — and deadly. Isn't that so?"

Reb Eliyahu and his son looked at Reb Shulem in amazement. Their glance said, "Is Reb Shulem also a prophet?"

"Thus the child's *hashkafah*, his way of looking at things, degenerated," Reb Shulem continued. "At quite a young age, he knew how to express himself on meaningful topics in a clear and pointed manner. He was a child who knew how to think like an adult, how to believe like an adult, and how to criticize the views of others like an adult, perhaps to an even greater degree.

"However, man's inclination is evil from his youth, and deadly criticism, even if it ultimately achieves the right goal and fills the positive regions in man's heart, is liable to arouse the malevolent region of his heart as well. One must be wary of voicing criticism, just as one must be extremely careful when using a very powerful drill. You can build with it but you can also kill with it.

"Right at the beginning of the year I noticed the force with which Asher was willing to hurt his friends. He was quite adept at denigrating and disgracing others. I didn't know where he had learned to do it.

"I first began to understand when I saw the cake he brought to the *cheder*. Quite casually, he made sure to tell his friends that his mother didn't rely on their parents' *hechsher*. Of course, there is a place for making sure that a child doesn't eat foods whose kashrus is uncertain. However, it is absolutely forbidden to give a child the feeling that this stems from contempt for others. What will a child raised that way absorb? What feelings will he incorporate?

"I saw that the boy was developing bad character traits but, because he was well aware of and afraid of the criticism you would give him at home, he managed, in his clever and cunning manner, to manipulate things so that you would admire him for the very things for which he should have been censured. That's why, instead of attacking his friends and lording over them in regular ways, he preferred to do it using a "spiritual" pretext, and about this our Sages have said, '*naval bi'reshus haTorah*.'

"I was the only one to notice it, and when I mentioned it to him, my words penetrated directly to his soul. Had I been his father or his rebbe, I am nearly certain that I would have overcome all obstacles, gotten all those responsible for him to join forces with me in order to put up roadblocks to his evil path and to redirect him, while utilizing the vast amount of material he absorbed — yes, and he did absorb a lot — in a positive direction.

"However, you didn't accept what I had to say. In your eyes, I was a simple '*schreiber*.' As part of your critical attitude, which contains more than a trace of pride, you failed to fulfill the dictum: 'From all who have taught me I have grown wise.' You did not think, or perhaps did not want to think, that a simple '*schreiber*' could show you what others did not notice. As a result, I found myself in the position of the one who was ruining things instead of the one who was repairing them. The backing and support which the child received at home proved to him that the path he had chosen would succeed. He was, of course, careful not to antagonize me again but, as I understand it, and I have been following his development over the years as I do with each and every one of my students, he has continued along that same path until this very day.

"Think," Reb Shulem told Reb Eliyahu, "how many people were ever portrayed in your home in a positive light? As worthy of admiration? Criticism of most of the educational authorities was voiced in your home, and the minute a child is raised and educated in such an atmosphere, with the understanding that it is conceivable to express venomous, sharp criticism against a teacher, educator or rebbe, why shouldn't he criticize his father, too?

"This is the reason that Asher's friends, those who come from relatively ordinary homes, are more G-d-fearing than he is. 'Awe of your teacher should be like your awe of Heaven,' and when a person is accustomed to criticizing those bigger than himself there is no telling how far he will go, while the simple, good-hearted students, who are taught to respect those who study Torah and not to denigrate them, grow up with healthier attitudes toward themselves and their surroundings. The fact that you have come to me indicates that you, too, Reb Eliyahu, have reached the same conclusion. Is that not so?"

Reb Eliyahu looked at Reb Shulem, and then back at his son, who was listening attentively to his former teacher, and he realized immediately that the truth lay with Reb Shulem. He recalled his own past behavior, his habit of disparaging anyone who disagreed with his way of thinking. He remembered how he had been secretly delighted when Asher had copied him exactly in his attitude of deprecation and scorn of things unworthy. Suddenly he understood. All of a sudden he felt a deep need to rush home and tell his entire family that he had made a mistake. Who knows? Perhaps his other children would take the same path! True, of all of them Asher was the sharpest. He knew how to criticize; he knew how to express his opinion and discredit the views of another — which definitely explained his behavior towards his father.

A long silence prevailed. At last Reb Eliyahu said, "What should we do now?"

"Do you trust me?" Reb Shulem asked.

"Of course," Reb Eliyahu assured him. "I can see it with my own eyes."

"Return to your studies and leave Asher here. Do you agree, Asher?"

Asher nodded willingly. He realized that it was this very same *"schreiber"* who would be able to help him out of the net he was caught up in, emotionally and spiritually, and who might even be able to somehow make his complicated relationship with his father "okay."

At four o'clock in the morning, the two — an elderly man of seventy and a fifteen-year-old youth — could be seen standing in the doorway of the shul, laughing like children. Their eyes were tired yet content. A relieved expression covered the young boy's face, and a victorious and pleased one, the elderly man's. At this point, he already knew that he had removed the obstacles which had accumulated on the path he had begun to build to the boy's heart three years before. Now all he had to do was to embark on the long but certain journey toward the depths of Asher's heart.

❧ Epilogue

This is a true story. Details have been changed to hide the identity of the real protagonists. Today "Asher" is today studying in a *yeshivah gedolah*. With Hashem's help, he overcame, although not without difficulty, the hurdle which stood to topple his spiritual world. The conversation with the *"schreiber"* and those which followed it, opened a line of communication between him and his father and eliminated the large amount of poison which had accumulated inside him all those years, allowing him to relax.

From a caustic young man, who used his acrid tongue to castigate his fellow man, Asher turned into a sensitive boy who gave to himself as well as those around him. Asher then began to build himself through working on his *middos* in his return to the Torah world.